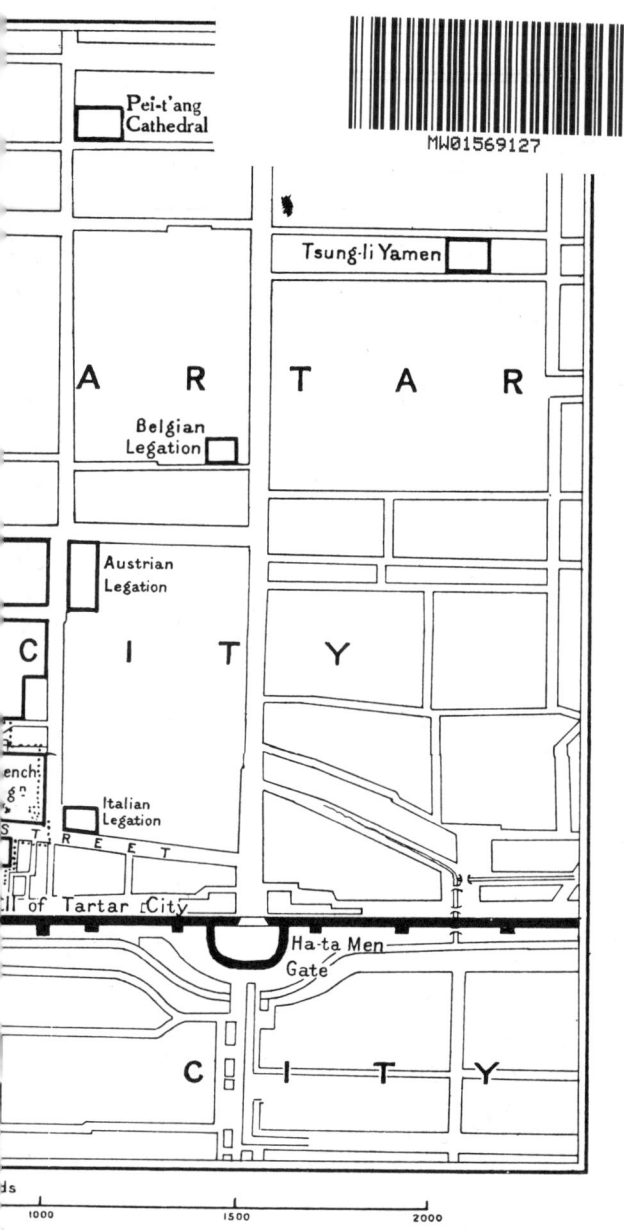

Photo, Elliott & Fry

SIR ROBERT HART

Frontispiece

BEHIND THE SCENES
IN PEKING

BEHIND THE SCENES IN PEKING

Mary Hooker

With an Introduction by H. J. Lethbridge

HONG KONG OXFORD NEW YORK
OXFORD UNIVERSITY PRESS
1987

Oxford University Press

Oxford   New York   Toronto
Petaling Jaya   Singapore   Hong Kong   Tokyo
Delhi   Bombay   Calcutta   Madras   Karachi
Nairobi   Dar es Salaam   Cape Town
Melbourne   Auckland

and associated companies in
Beirut   Berlin   Ibadan   Nicosia

Introduction   ©   Oxford University Press

First published by John Murray (Publishers) Ltd. London 1910
This edition reprinted, with permission and with the addition
of an Introduction in Oxford Paperbacks 1987

All rights reserved. No part of this publication may be reproduced,
stored in a retrieval system, or transmitted, in any form or by any
means, electronic, mechanical, photocopying, recording, or otherwise,
without the prior permission of Oxford University Press

ISBN 0 19 584208 1

OXFORD is a trade mark of Oxford University Press

Printed in Hong Kong by Kings Time Printing Press Ltd.
Published by Oxford University Press, Warwick House, Hong Kong

INTRODUCTION

ON 28 May 1900, two American women, standing on the balcony of a converted temple in the Western Hills of Chihli (Zhili), were startled to see flames and smoke rising from the railway station and foreign settlement at Fengtai. The women were Mrs Squiers, the wife of the First Secretary of the American Legation, and her guest from Japan, the young and pretty Polly Condit Smith (Mary Hooker). As they watched, perplexed and alarmed by the conflagration, from the direction of the blaze a horseman came cantering up, like a knight errant. The rider was Dr G.E. Morrison, *The Times* correspondent in Peking (Beijing), who had come to warn them of dangers from marauding Boxers. Soon after, up rode Mrs Squiers' husband, Herbert, on a similar mission, escorted by a Cossack guard.

The party of European men, women, and children,

together with their Chinese servants, spent an anxious night in the temple. Early next morning they departed for Peking, to the apparent sanctuary of the Legations. Polly Condit Smith was not to know, as she arrived thankfully at the American Legation, that soon she and over three thousand people would remain beleaguered in the Legation compound for 55 terrifying days, days filled with events which would outrage the civilized world and, for a decade or so, largely shape China's international relations.

The Boxer movement originated in the Shantung (Shandong) peninsula, and from there spread to other northern Chinese provinces. Boxers were mostly peasants and appeared at first as almost leaderless bands bent on hunting down missionaries and their Chinese converts, whom they stigmatized as 'secondary devils'. They were distinguished by their flaming red sashes, their superstitions and trances, and by their ferocious courage, for they believed in their invulnerability to bullet, shot and shell, and the thrust of the bayonet. The Boxer Uprising, as Western historians term this outbreak, may best be described as a nativistic or populist movement (a type of Jacquerie) whose targets were not, however, the Chinese upper

INTRODUCTION

stratum or propertied classes but foreigners and their Chinese Christian converts. It is true that Boxers had an exaggerated hatred for foreigners and all their works in China, but at that time — the turn of the century — so had most Chinese people in varying degrees, for Imperial China appeared to be breaking up as a result of both Western penetration and pressure, and Japanese aggression. In social psychological terms, the Boxers were animated by a fear that the world they knew was being lost to them by the malign activities of outsiders. Consequently, Boxers were xenophobic and conservative; they were rebels, but not revolutionaries.

Surviving a siege depends primarily on four interrelated factors: defences, provisions, morale, and relief (unless of course the besiegers simply fold up their tents and depart). The Legation Quarter (as it later became known) formed a fairly compact, roughly quadrilateral area once the outlying Austrian, Belgian, Danish, and Italian Legations had been abandoned and the ornamental park abutting the British Legation had been taken over. In this ornamental park lay the palace of Prince Su, which had been garrisoned by the Japanese under the valiant Colonel Shiba, one of the quiet heroes of the siege (Polly Condit Smith describes him as 'a splendid, small fellow'). A section of the Tartar City Wall which overlooked the Quarter had also been seized, and proved to be a vantage point of great strategic value for the defenders.

Self-help, ingenuity, and improvisation are important in any successful defence. This was so at Mafeking, a town which, encircled by Boers, held out for seven months until a relief column arrived. There, the English under Major Baden-Powell, constructed a six-inch gun and refurbished another — a smoothbore, muzzle-loading naval gun, manufactured in 1770. In Peking, after the start of the siege, the polyglot troops hastily sent to protect the European civilians possessed four pieces of artillery. There was a fifth, a Russian field-gun, which should have gone but had inadvertently been left behind in the confusion. None the less its ammunition had been brought along. An old gun with a rifled barrel, probably a relic of the Anglo-French expedition of 1860, was discovered in a foundry and mounted on a spare pair of wheels. Providentially, the ammunition destined for the absent Russian gun suited its calibre. The resurrected gun did sterling work in demolishing Chinese barricades on the Tartar City Wall and stuffed with assorted metal pieces it became deadly at close quarters.

One refugee was an American missionary called Gamewell, who had trained as an engineer. Gamewell was appointed head of the Fortification Committee and together with his coadjutors worked strenuously throughout the siege to improve defences and construct bomb-proof shelters. Peter Fleming in his account of the siege declares: 'There was probably no single individual to whom the besieged became more deeply indebted.' The role of a military engineer is not just to build defence works against attack but to reduce casualties among the besieged. Like the Russian engineer, Todleben, at the 11-month siege of Sebastopol, Gamewell did his best to protect the soldiers, marines, and civilians within the lines. However, in time the sheer attrition of the garrison, the steady loss and incapacitation of fighting men, would have nullified his art but that point was never reached as relief arrived just in time.

Ancient and medieval sieges usually ended when the garrisons of castles or fortified places began to suffer from starvation and pestilence. In those days, there were no canned goods, no effective medicines, and few survived surgery. The decisive factor was always food, and continued to be so in the nineteenth century. At Vicksburg, in 1863, during the American Civil War, resolution weakened and morale slumped when flour reached US$1,000 a barrel, meat US$250 a pound, and the garrison was reduced to eating one mouldy biscuit a day, bringing about the turning point, when Vicksburg surrendered to General Grant.

One is bemused to read in Polly Condit Smith's book: 'Mrs Squiers has a large supply of champagne and every night we have one or two quarts with our siege dinner.' But the various legations had well-stocked cellars, and diplomatists did themselves well in Peking, for Imbeck's and Kierulff's (shops in the Legation Quarter) both had large stocks of French wines, various delicacies, and tobacco. The Hôtel de Pékin, adjacent to the French Legation, also had ample supplies of the same, and other luxuries. Throughout the siege men (and some women who smoked incessantly from boredom or nervousness) could puff on their cigars and cheroots and relax with a stiff whisky and soda or glass of wine. This was a situation not typical of most sieges.

Food, to begin with, was in plentiful supply — Imbeck's, Kierulff's, and neighbouring rice shops provided excellent larders; but towards the end, after the herd of sheep had been slaughtered, the staple diet for the besieged was horse-meat and rice, made palatable with the addition of curry powder. The Chinese Christians, who had been brought into the Legation Quarter by the intercession of the compassionate Morrison, had mostly to fend for themselves and ate cats and dogs when these could be found. Nearly all of those who died from malnutrition or starvation were babies and young children, for there was practically no supply of fresh milk.

The morale of the besieged was much affected by the tide of rumour, by vague stories that the allied forces were close to, or distant from Peking, or had not advanced a step from Tientsin (Tianjin). In the early days, spirits rose when a sentry saw a green rocket rushing up in the distant sky; stories would then circulate that a Russian force was hurrying to their rescue; the next day excited Russians claimed to have heard '*les sonneries du canon*' of the approaching troops. There were level-headed, sanguine men like Morrison who did much to sustain morale by his good sense and cool demeanour. There were also prophets of doom, neurasthenics, hysterics, and the plainly mad. The French Minister, Pichon, was a prophet of doom — a highly excitable, volatile creature.

Polly Condit Smith records that he 'nervously and ceaselessly' walked about exclaiming: '*La situation est excessivement grave; nous allons tous mourir ce soir.*' Morrison, in his diaries, bluntly states that Pichon was a 'poltroon'.

Sir Robert Hart, the feline and equivocal Inspector-General of Chinese Customs, had spent nearly all his life in China, but still remained perplexed by that country's admittedly convoluted and arcane politics. At times he was prepared to believe, against all reason, in the good intentions of the Court and Yamen officials. He gave dubious advice to the foreign diplomatists, immured in the various Legations. But his trump card was that he had lived longer in China than practically anyone else, and that therefore he *knew* the Chinese mind. Polly Condit Smith found him kind, charming, and a trifle vain — a bit of a 'pussycat' — who took malicious pleasure, so it seemed, in alarming his auditors. On the contrary Morrison did not have such a high opinion of Hart.

The besieged could only be saved by outside intervention; in time food and ammunition would run out and it was thought the Boxer hordes and Chinese troops would swarm into the Legation Quarter and then massacre every man, woman, and child. They remembered the Indian Mutiny and the dreadful fate of those trapped and slaughtered at Cawnpore. Books on the mutiny, copies of which were found in the British and American Legations, were much read and provoked, one imagines, many a nasty *frisson*. Relief was slow in coming because the Allies had to overwhelm the Taku (Dagu) forts and then assemble in Tientsin. It took some time to get everything shipshape and collect supplies. An international force is notoriously difficult to govern and there was much wrangling between the various national commanders, each of whom wanted to be in the vanguard. The first troops that Polly Condit Smith saw in the flesh were Sikhs. A little blonde Englishwoman, she tells us, was so overcome that she threw her arms around one and embraced him. The turbanned Sikh was dumbfounded: it was not quite the thing for memsahibs to do in those caste-conscious days.

But what of Polly Condit Smith herself, a young American *en vacance* in China, caught up in these extraordinary events? She is remarkably like a Henry James heroine — observant, amused, wry, yet withal innocent. She was quick to spot the funny and the incongruous. She relates that von Below, the German chargé d'affaires, whom she liked, played music from

Wagner's *Die Walküre* during what he thought was to be the final Boxer onslaught, and thus prepared himself on the piano for suitable entry into the next world Von Below, a Nietzschean one feels, beyond good and evil, was always a little stagy in her eyes. She records a nice story of Mrs Conger, the American Minister's wife, who once found Polly lying on her bed *en déshabillé*. 'Do you want to be found undressed when the end comes?' Polly replied that she was going to stay in bed unless something terrible happened, 'when I should don my dressing-gown and, with a pink bow at my throat, await my massacre'. 'I must say', she adds, 'that at some terrible moments during the siege it is a great comfort to be frivolous.' This Mrs Conger was a fervent disciple of Mary Baker Eddy, the founder of Christian Science, and had once lectured a group of women on the unreality, or the impalpable nature, of the bullets whizzing around them. They were told that 'while there was an appearance of warlike hostilities, it was really in our own brains'.

In recorded history there have been many sieges and the more celebrated — Constantinople, Malta, Vienna, Gibralter, for example — have been much written about in diaries and memoirs or in mono-

INTRODUCTION

graphs and histories. The sieges of the Indian Mutiny have given rise to an extensive literature and, in fiction, to at least one good novel — J.G. Farrell's *The Siege of Krishnapur*. The investment of the Peking Legations has also acquired a large bibliography and one of the better first-hand accounts — perhaps the best — is that by Polly Condit Smith. It is compiled from letters written but not sent and from passages taken from her diaries. Published in England and America ten years after the events, it is a cool look at the past, at the terrifying experiences of a young woman marooned in the Legations.

We do not know what changes or what deletions she made in the original texts, but she must have exercised some censorship over her material to remove comments too uninhibited or uncharitable, or too cutting or catty, for Morrison's published diaries reveal the nastier, murkier side of the siege, and in so doing he removed the gilt from many a diplomatic reputation. The siege had its saints and sinners, and the brave and lively Polly.

H.J. LETHBRIDGE

BIBLIOGRAPHY

Allen, Revd Roland, *The Siege of the Peking Legations* (London, Smith, Elder & Co, 1901).

Coltman, Robert, *Beleaguered in Peking* (Philadelphia, F.A. Davis Co, 1901).

Fleming, Peter, *The Siege at Peking* (London, Rupert Hart-Davis, 1959).

Martin, W.A.P., *The Siege in Peking* (Edinburgh, Oliphant Andrews & Ferrier, 1900).

Oliphant, Nigel, *A Diary of the Siege of the Legations in Peking* (London, Longmans & Co, 1901).

Pichon, Stéphen, *Dans la Bataille* (Paris, A. Méricant, 1908).

Putnam Weale, B.L. (Bertram Lenox Simpson), *Indiscreet Letters from Peking* (London, Hurst & Blackett, 1907).

Purcell, Victor, *The Boxer Uprising* (Cambridge, Cambridge University Press, 1963).

BIBLIOGRAPHY

Russell, S.M., *The Story of the Siege in Peking* (London, Elliot Stock, 1901).

Smith, Arthur H., *China in Convulsion* (Edinburgh, Oliphant & Co, 1901).

Tan, Chester C., *The Boxer Catastrophe* (New York, Columbia University Press, 1955).

BEHIND THE SCENES IN PEKING

BEING EXPERIENCES DURING THE
SIEGE OF THE LEGATIONS

BY MARY HOOKER

WITH ILLUSTRATIONS

LONDON
JOHN MURRAY, ALBEMARLE STREET, W.
1910

PREFACE

It does not fall to the lot of every woman—or man, either—to go through a siege, especially one so remarkable, and, indeed, unique in many of its features, as that of the Legations in Peking.

The feeling that my experiences were out of the common, and present new aspects of famous events, during which I was, to a certain extent, at the same time on the stage and behind the scenes, has induced me to publish the following pages. They are taken from letters, owing to circumstances never sent, and my diary, written spasmodically throughout the siege. While trying to introduce something of the lighter side of life, and speaking of various incidents, humorous and otherwise, I have endeavoured to avoid all that can give offence or displeasure to those mentioned.

PREFACE

If in any case I have unwittingly failed in this endeavour, I crave pardon.

My thanks are due to Mrs. Woodward for giving permission to reproduce her unique siege photographs.

MARY HOOKER.

September, 1910.

LIST OF ILLUSTRATIONS

	TO FACE PAGE
SIR ROBERT HART	*frontispiece*
WHITE PAGODA IN THE TEMPLE OF LINGUA SU	2
HERBERT SQUIERS	14
RUSSIAN MARINE GUARD CAPTAIN McCALLA COMMANDING THE AMERICAN MARINES	16
CH'IEN MEN GATE	24
BARON VON KETTELER	26
BARRICADE BETWEEN THE AMERICAN AND RUSSIAN LEGATIONS READING THE SENTENCE OF DEATH TO THE BOXERS CAUGHT IN THE RUSSIAN LEGATION	30
THE TSUNG-LI YAMEN	44
BARRICADE ACROSS THE CANAL TO THE FU SANDBAG BARRICADE IN AMERICAN LEGATION	50
MRS. R. S. HOOKER	68
CAPTAIN JOHN T. MYERS	100
MRS. SQUIERS	110
LOADING THE "INTERNATIONAL" AMERICAN AND RUSSIAN MARINES AT WORK ON THE BARRICADE. BARON VON RAHDEN ON THE RIGHT	116
SIR CLAUDE MACDONALD	120
EDWIN H. CONGER	136

viii LIST OF ILLUSTRATIONS

	TO FACE PAGE
A GATE INTO THE IMPERIAL CITY	154
GENERAL A. R. CHAFFEE	160
GENERAL SIR ALFRED GASELEE	176
THE RESULT OF THE SIEGE: IN THE AMERICAN MINISTER'S HOUSE	192
THE RESULT OF THE SIEGE: FRENCH LEGATION RUINS	
MRS. HOOKER, MISS ARMSTRONG, LADY MACDONALD'S LITTLE GIRLS, FARGO SQUIERS, AND COLONEL ARTHUR CHURCHILL	196
COAL HILL	202

BEHIND THE SCENES IN PEKING

May 26, 1900.

WHEN you were in Peking last year I don't know whether you got out to the hills or not. They are about fifteen miles from the imperial city, and are the nearest point where foreigners can find relief from the insufferable heat of the capital, which begins with an intensely hot spring, continuing through a long, damp, sizzling summer.

Many of the diplomats have cottages and bungalows at Pei-ta-ho, on the seashore, but its distance from Peking is a great drawback to it as a summer residence, and they have been forced to accept the hills, as a nearer and more practical place for their summer colony.

A large, commodious house has been built here for the British Minister, as well as one for the officials of the Customs, both within their respective compounds. The greater part of this colony, how-

2   BEHIND THE SCENES IN PEKING

ever, have simply leased temples from Buddhist priests, and converted them into the most attractive and livable summer homes, the American and Russian Legations being the principal of these.

A huge, white pagoda, belonging to the temple of Linqua Su, in the centre of this district, with its temples of Buddha and houses of its priests surrounding it, is perched on the top of a hill at the base of Mount Bruce, and for miles around is the most picturesque feature of the landscape. In the highest point of this pagoda is hung a wonderful bell, the only motive-power of which is the wind, and which was placed there by the Chinese to frighten the evil spirits of the air. When the breeze is strong, which is often the case, the bell seems to thresh itself into a veritable fury, and again at midday, when the breeze is light, one can just distinguish the faintest tinkle.

High up in these hills, and built on the sides of Mount Bruce, stand these temples with their subordinate and associated buildings, each making up a separate community. Ours is some-what above the temple of Linqua Su, with its white

WHITE PAGODA IN THE TEMPLE OF LINGUA SU

OUR TEMPLE HOME

pagoda, and is built on a most wonderful natural shelf of the mountain-side. A terrace, edged by a low, ivy-covered parapet, runs the length of our temple home, from which we look right out on the world beneath us, down the valley towards Peking; or, if we look above us, it is to see Mount Bruce rise perpendicularly against the sky. Ancient and big are the stones that pave the outer and inner courts of this temple, and as picturesque as they are difficult to use are the stone steps, formed of heavy and irregular slabs, which lead down to the valley or ascend up unto the mountain, from which steps finally emerge innumerable tracks, leading in their turn to shrines, homes of hermits, and temples built on this continuous ridge. Nor is this barbaric and ancient setting for a modern life made less extraordinary by the fact that one is served by quiet, intelligent, besatined servants, who glide about and look as if they had stepped into life straight from the half-fabulous days of Kubla Khan; and you feel they have always been thus, and always will be, and you wonder how it is that although the spirit of the twentieth century is certainly felt in China, it is little seen.

May 27.

To-day we started off on a long tramp, making first the ascent of Mount Bruce, which was so difficult at times that we could scarcely accomplish it, and had we not had the help of a young house-servant, known to us as " Number Three Boy," I doubt if we could have reached the summit. The wind whistled round the high peaks of Mount Bruce to such an extent that Mrs. Squiers and I had to hold on to each other to keep from being blown off our feet.

From here we could see the Empress Dowager's summer palace and grounds, spread out below us like a toy garden, with its wonderful landscape effects and its series of artificial water-ways. Then, perched high up on a mountain, we could see a white temple belonging to the eunuchs of the palace, and reserved solely for their use during the summer months; and to the west the Feng-tai station of the Peking-Paoting-fu Railway, winding through the valleys below us like a piece of grey thread. We then walked through the enclosure of the temple occupied by the Russian Legation, and in passing through a half shrine, half summer-house, most unexpectedly

CHINESE SHEPHERDS

came to a wall upon which was drawn a rough but cleverly executed head of a lovely young girl. It was done in coloured pastels, and had been drawn by some artist diplomat. The subject was the Countess Marguerite Cassini, niece of the Russian Minister, who had been stationed in Peking some years previous. It was a beautiful bit of work, and was especially startling when seen surrounded by the hideous, grinning faces of Buddhist gods.

Heading for our own temple of Linqua Su, we walked miles, keeping to the top of a ridge, where the views were gorgeous and the air wonderful, and quite suddenly came upon a shepherd and his flock. Fancy it, a Chinese shepherd tending his Chinese sheep! His expression was gentler and happier by far than that of men leading a like monotonous existence in the mountains of Switzerland or elsewhere in the West. Could it be that there the shepherd longs to return to the life in the villages, while here the life of the poorest classes in the village communities is so hopeless a struggle that individual members are glad to leave the hopelessness of it and tend their flocks alone upon the mountains? This fascinating China! you have been here, and you know it. I must not bore you with my impressions, for if I attempted such a thing these letters to you would assume the proportions of an encyclopædia.

May 27 (continued).

Mr. Squiers returned to the American Legation this morning. He only gets out to the hills twice a week in time to dine and returns to Peking the following morning. He tells us that the Boxers daily become more daring, but the diplomats and people in general put these things down to the usual spring riots which yearly seize Peking, and are due to hunger and disease, prevalent among the poorer classes after a long, hard winter. Nevertheless, it was deemed wise to inform the Tsung-li Yamen (the Foreign Office) that we were in the hills at the temple of Linqua Su, and would expect official protection from all rioters or malcontents who might be in this region, and a guard of twelve Chinese soldiers was promptly detailed to protect "nos personnes et nos biens." But *such* soldiers!—opera-bouffe mannikins in a Broadway theatre would frighten one with their martial air compared to these ridiculous apologies for soldiers,

BOXERS AND THEIR MOTTO

which were sent to us for our protection, their only weapons being dull-pointed rusty spears!

Clara, the German governess, returned from Peking to-day, where she had gone to do some shopping, and tells us that all the natives she passed seemed to be armed, and that in all the temple enclosures companies of Chinese were being drilled.

Our servants, mostly native Christians, assure us that these people are all Boxers, most of them flaunting the red sash, the insignia of that Society, and that they are preparing for a general uprising when the time shall be ripe—an uprising that has for its watchword, "Death and destruction to the foreigner and all his works, and loyal support to the great Ching dynasty."

May 28.

The peace that settles on one after a long tramp in the mountains was rudely broken up for us a short while after our return from our walk yesterday, when we found ourselves thrown into the midst of a most exciting situation, from which we knew the chances were about even whether we should escape with our lives.

We could see from our mountain balcony that

the railroad station at Feng-tai, with its foreign settlement, was burning. The immense steel bridge was gone, too, showing that dynamite and high explosives had been used to destroy it. The locality was thick with smoke and the flames sky-high. Our servants told us our highly picturesque guard of twelve had run away as soon as they were sure the Boxers were burning Feng-tai, for, they argued, the mob will surely sack this foreign-devil temple when they finish with Feng-tai. Since they had begun, they certainly would not desist until everything foreign this side of Peking was sacked and burned, and this guard had no desire to pose as the guardians of foreigners, but thought it much safer to join the so far victorious rabble at Feng-tai. We also learned that over a hundred men engaged in agricultural and other peaceful occupations in and around the temples, of which ours was one, had left during the day to join the Boxers.

Our position now, to say the least, was critical. Not a foreign man on the place to protect us; a quantity of badly frightened Chinese servants to reassure; three children, their governesses and ourselves, to make plans for. We did what women

DR. MORRISON TO THE RESCUE

always have to do—we waited; and our reward came when we saw down in the valley a dusty figure ambling along on a dusty Chinese pony, coming from the direction of Feng-tai and making direct for our temple. It was Dr. Morrison, correspondent of the London *Times*, and an intimate friend of the Squierses.

On hearing early in the day of the mob at Feng-tai, and the burning of the place, he promptly started off in that direction to get as near as possible to the scene of action, and ascertain for himself if the wild rumours circulating in Peking were truths before cabling them to London. Finding the worst corroborated by what he saw from a point near the mob, yet unseen by it, he started on his return trip to Peking, hot haste for the cable office, when he became oppressed with the startling remembrance that we were at the temple, and probably alone and unprotected. So, instead of returning to Peking, he promptly came to us. He feared lest Mr. Squiers had not heard of the burning of Feng-tai, or, if he had heard of it, that possibly the city gates might be closed against the approaching mob, and he might be unable to leave the capital that night. The fact that our temple was directly on the line of march to Peking for the rioters made it look to Dr. Morrison as a most probable possibility that they would stop *chez nous* before proceeding to the capital. In case of such horrible eventuality he hoped to defend us for a while, and to send to glory as many Chinese as possible before turning up his own toes!

He was studying a possible defence of our balcony-home when Mr. Squiers arrived post-haste, bringing with him a Russian Cossack, whom he had borrowed from the Russian Minister. Plans were now made to defend the place from attack or incendiaries during the night. The Chinese servants worked with a will—our successful defence meant safety for us and life for them. Sentry work of the most careful sort continued all night, as well as the packing up of our clothes and valuables.

At 6 a.m. we were *en route* for Peking—an enormous caravan—most of us in Chinese carts, some riding ponies, mules, or donkeys, the forty servants placing themselves wherever they could—*anywhere*, in fact—so that they should not be left behind. The three protectors, heavily armed, rode by us, and three or four of the Chinese were armed also, and the carts held such a position in the caravan that in a moment they could be swung round as a defence in case of an attack.

The fifteen miles through which we travelled were utterly deserted except for the long, lonely lines of coal-carrying dromedaries. It seemed as if the country people *en masse* had deserted their villages and gone to some rallying-point for a demonstration; and how anxiously and slowly each half-hour of the trip passed, for, while it brought us nearer to our Legation, it also brought us nearer to the possibility that our caravan would run into yesterday's rioters with added numbers of to-day's malcontents.

At 10.30 we reached the American Legation compound, and most painfully but thankfully we untwisted ourselves from the awful position we were forced to take in the cart, and joyously grasped the hands of friends. William Pethick, Li Hung Chang's private secretary for twenty years, a person of tremendous influence with the Chinese, was in the compound, and was on the point of going to the War Office to demand a regiment to go with him to our rescue out in the hills. He had feared for us desperately during the night following the burning of Feng-tai.

May 30.

The times have become so dangerous that no women are allowed to leave the compound, but, of course, the diplomats and the military—such as are here—must move about and try to find out what the situation really is. The people who know the most about it are the most pessimistic as to what may happen before the marines arrive from Tien-tsin.

We were glad to hear that the Belgian officials at the Feng-tai station had heard of the intentions of the Chinese to burn them and the place, and had escaped to Peking without loss of life.

All the Legations that have battleships at Taku wired some days ago to them, and we are looking for a total of about three hundred marines of all nationalities to reach Peking at any moment.

Legations, such as the Belgian and Austrian, which are some distance from the Legation centre, are forced to do constant sentry work to guard against thieves and incendiaries; the Ministers' secretaries, and their foreign servants take turn night and day. They are so surrounded by small streets and alleys that a few rioters could rush their Legations easily, and they are forced to keep the most alert watch. Melotte, the big blonde Belgian secretary, came to tea to-day, and gave us a most vivid description of the difficulties of their tiny garrison.

Sir Robert Hart, the beloved Inspector-General of the Customs, dropped in also, and, while he seems fairly sanguine about the present situation, I must say the tales of China and the Chinese that he unfolded to us were quite terrible. Especially the massacre of the Portuguese at Ning-po in 1870 by the Chinese in retaliation for their having taken so much of the Yangtse River trade made a stirring story when coming from his lips.

He was with that fascinating Englishman commonly known as "Chinese Gordon" when he was the central figure in the history of China during the early part of this century, and when Sir Robert was quite a young man. I was so obviously spellbound by these real reminiscences that, to my surprise and joy, he offered to send me, on his return to his compound, a photograph of himself taken with Gordon, marked with the latter's autograph. I can't say, however, that his visit reassured us in our present dangerous situation.

Before leaving he looked at Mr. Squiers's

wonderful collection of antique Chinese porcelains, which Mr. Pethick, a connoisseur in these things, has collected for him. The Dana Collection was also procured by him. Sir Robert is certainly a delightful person, and the cobalt-blue tie twisted into a most unusual knot around his low collar gives his personal appearance a tinge of rakishness and eccentricity.

This afternoon Dr. Morrison and some Customs students rode down toward the station of Magi-poo to take a look at the congested market-places and collections of angry rioters. Directly they were seen they were furiously stoned, but as their Chinese ponies were fleet of foot, they escaped with a few bruises.

May 31.

All day to-day everyone is wondering, " Will the marines get here to-night?" A wire came through Admiral Kempff, saying they were entrained. Last night we dined at Sir R. Hart's, and danced until twelve. He has two bands, brass and string, of Chinese musicians whom he has taught. The secretary of the German Legation took me out to dinner—Von Below, a most soldierly-looking person.

HERBERT SQUIERS

To face page 14

ARRIVAL OF TROOPS

June 1.

Mr. Squiers, secretary of the Legation, and Mr. Cheshire, interpreter-secretary, met the troops at the station last night at 8.30. The marines of the United States, England, Russia, France, and Japan, formed the contingent of 365 men which were sent up from Tien-tsin by the fleet. They would have arrived earlier in the day, but the British in Tientsin had tried to send 100 marines instead of the 75 for which the Tsung-li Yamen had given them permission. The Chinese were obdurate, so the delay was caused.

When this polyglot contingent landed at the station in Peking there was great excitement as to which nationality should lead. Captain McCalla, who had come up with our fifty marines, hurried his men at the double-quick to get it, and our troops were the first to march up Legation Street. There was an enormous mob at the station, but no demonstration was made except to hurl and howl curses on the soldiers' ancestors.

Mr. Squiers, who is one of the most hospitable people in the world, received Captain McCalla and the marine officers in a delightful manner, and did everything possible for them in an official and personal way. He was an officer in the army before entering the diplomatic service, which makes his help and advice invaluable in procuring quarters for the marines, and other arrangements.

June 3.

Yesterday Captain McCalla took the eleven o'clock train, with his secretary, back to Tien-tsin, to join his ship, the *Newark,* after having had a long talk discussing the situation with the Minister. We suppose Admiral Kempff will be up in a day or two, as his visit has been put off already several times.

The bad and suspicious part of this affair is that the Boxer outrages are not being punished by the Government, which proves that they either fear the perpetrators or sympathize with them. One hears from all sides that the Chinese soldiers are Boxers at heart, and would not fire on them if ordered to do so. The people who will suffer first from these riotous fanatics, if they get much worse than they are now, will be the Chinese Christians.

The heat is becoming insufferable, and the children of the diplomatic corps are showing the bad effects of this enforced confinement. The

RUSSIAN MARINE GUARD

Copyright, M. S. Woodward

CAPTAIN McCALLA, COMMANDING THE AMERICAN MARINES

To face page 16

RAILWAY DIFFICULTIES

British Minister's wife, Lady Macdonald, has sent her little girls back to their legation bungalow in the hills, in the care of her charming sister, Miss Armstrong, with a guard of thirty marines. We cannot solve the problem in our Legation this way, as our guard is so much smaller.

June 5.

We expected Admiral Kempff yesterday from Tien-tsin, but the train did not come through, and we do not know whether he was on it or not. The invitations for a dinner in his honour have been cancelled.

Mrs. Brent, with whom I am to return to Japan, has sent me word to be ready to-morrow to take the morning train to Tien-tsin. So far all the trains from Peking down seem to get through, although the trains up are irregular. Rumour comes that yesterday two more stations were burnt, one on the Hankow line and one on the Tien-tsin line, but the actual tracks are not destroyed.

Everyone feels that this is the time to leave Peking—everyone, at least, who is not bound to remain to protect interests they have in charge— and to-morrow surely the exodus will be large. Captain Myers, in command of the United States marines, and Captain Strouts, of the British marines, had a long consultation to-day about these incredibly outrageous Boxers, in case they should dare impertinences on the Legations. Should we be forced to leave our American compound, we will go to the Russian Legation, which has a stronger defensive position than ours.

June 7.

Yesterday I was ready to start with Mrs. Brent, when a letter came for Mrs. Squiers from Sir Robert Hart, saying he thought the train would eventually "get through" to Tien-tsin, but that his secret service agents had informed him that there were rioters and Boxers at several stations prepared to stone the passenger coaches, and he urged me not to attempt the trip. He wrote: "Things must get better soon or very much worse."

Captain Myers and his men were up all night guarding the compound. This United States Legation is such a wretched little irregular place to defend—it could so easily be fired.

The atmosphere of the compound is distinctly exciting. The quintessence of American interests are discussed right here in the open air, under a few scattered big trees, by people walking about

IMPENDING DANGER

gesticulating or standing on scorching hot flagstones, which pave part of this enclosure, arguing with one another as to how soon the *coup d'état* will take place, but all agreeing on one point—that a cable should be sent immediately to the State Department in Washington before telegraphic communication is lost; that nothing but a tremendous armed force can free the Americans in Peking from a surely approaching massacre; that many of the higher Chinese officials would try to protect us to the end. But the fact remains, if the Boxers and rioters continue to increase in numbers each day as they have been doing for the past week, it will be the mob we will have to deal with, and not the Tsung-li Yamen.

In nearly every instance the persons who voice these sentiments are men who have lived in China for years, who know the country, the language, and the people. They know that the strength of the Chinese lies in clever cunning and mob violence, that they cannot be trusted under any circumstances.

These men all agree that China was never before in such a condition. Mr. Pethick, familiar with every phase of tortuous Chinese government, forty years a resident in China, and an intimate friend of half the political leaders, knowing their weaknesses and wickednesses by heart, urges the Minister to state to Washington the situation as it is, but all to no avail.

The white dazzling star of optimism is blinding him to facts, and with the British Minister to stand with him in his position, he says that the Boxer movement is only a few fanatics, and the mobs and incendiaries are but slight demonstrations of the yearly spring riots !

Dr. Coltman, a clever American physician of Peking, and a correspondent for the *Chicago Record*, is sending to his paper some strong cables about affairs here, but the United States are so saturated with yellow journalism that probably his wires will not be believed. When we complain to the Yamen about the trains running no longer from Peking to Tien-tsin, as many ladies and children wish to leave, they smile and say "they regret the present state of affairs, but that in a few days all will be in working order again." Mr. Pethick thinks they are not allowing the trains to leave Tien-tsin because they don't want any more foreign troops to come to Peking.

TROOPS EXPECTED IN VAIN

June 10.

A telegram arrived to-day from Tien-tsin, saying the second contingent that they have been so madly telegraphing for these past few days had practically seized a train and left at 10.10, that most of the track is supposed to be all right, but they expect to have difficulty with an occational broken bridge. Captain McCalla is again in command of our marines, and the combined forces of this relief party number 1,600. We expect the train to arrive to-night, and, owing to the gates being closed at sundown, they will have to spend the night outside. To-morrow at daybreak they will be met with twenty carts for their ammunition and luggage.

June 11.

This morning Mr. Squiers, and Mr. Cheshire, and Captain Myers, with ten marines, waited at the station for the troops from daybreak until eleven o'clock, but there was no sign of them. The escort then returned to the Legation. The telegraph was broken last night. We have no more communication with the outside world; our world is this dangerous Peking.

June 12.

Such intense excitement! This afternoon the Japanese Chancellor of Legation went down to the railway-station in the official Legation cart to see if there were any sign of the troops. Returning by the principal gate, he was seized by Imperial troops, disembowelled, and cut to pieces.

Mr. Squiers had sent about the same hour his *maffu* (groom) down to the station with a pony for Captain McCalla in case the troops had come. This man was also returning, after having waited there some hours, when they—the Imperial Chinese soldiers—saw that he was some foreigner's servant, and tried to seize him, but he lashed both horses—the one he was on and the one he was leading—and just escaped. On reaching the Legation, he was so terrified he told Mr. Squiers he would have to leave his service immediately and try to save his life by running away to Tien-tsin.

Twenty of our marines have been sent with an officer to guard the big Methodist mission near the Ha Ta Men Gate, which is still holding out.

Rumours are the only subject of conversation now. To have them refuted or confirmed, a Russian bribed a reliable Chinese to go fifty miles

STILL NO TROOPS

down the track and to report where the troops are He could find no sign of them. How very extraordinary! Where are these 1,600 men that left Tien-tsin two days ago? He also reported that the track was broken in several places.

To-day the house belonging to the British Minister in the hills, very near our temple, was looted and burnt by the Boxers. Most fortunately, Miss Armstrong brought the children back yesterday.

A Russian secretary, Mr. Kroupensky, has figures at the end of his fingers about the number of troops Russia can land in Tien-tsin from Port Arthur in a few days' time, etc., and if things get much worse, the Russians say it is more than probable their people will march on to Peking by themselves to our rescue. Can we suppose they are trying to prepare us for a Russian *coup d'état*?

Dr. A. W. P. Martin, a famous savant in Chinese classics and other ancient languages, Director of the Imperial University in Peking, has temporarily become the refugee guest of Mr. Squiers, his own house being too unsafe for him to remain in. Mr. Pethick is also a guest in this hospitable house. The British Legation is already crammed with missionaries and refugees, who in their own quarters feared for their lives, and were obliged to leave their missions near Peking, and concentrate at some place capable of defence.

A message that has to be sent to the Tsung-li Yamen always gains more strength by being sent from each Legation the same day. To-day the Japanese were requested to join the others with this usual procedure, but they answered simply: " Impossible. The Chinese have murdered our Third Secretary of Legation, and Japan can have no more communication with China—except war."

June 13.

All last night the sky was bright from the many fires in the Tartar city—work done by the Boxers and soldiers. The Roman Catholic Church, the "Tungchou," was burnt to the ground, and all through the night the Christian Chinese who lived near it were massacred. Other less important missions have also been destroyed. Yesterday the people in the Austrian Legation rescued a Chinese Christian woman who was being burned to death very near their Legation wall.

Baron von Ketteler, the German Minister, con-

CH'IEN MEN GATE

MEASURES FOR DEFENCE

sidered some Boxer who walked down Legation Street was impertinent to him, and chased him up the street as far as the Russian Bank, where he finally captured him. He was beating him over the head with his walking-stick even before the fellow stopped, and the crowd that collected was enormous. Captain Myers, Captain Strouts of the English, and Baron von Rahden, of the Russian guard, seized this opportunity to make a kind of rush down and up Legation Street, placing the Maxim-gun ready to use if necessary, and in this way completely cleared it of Chinese from the Dutch Legation down to the Italian. They had wanted to take this step for some time, deeming it has now become necessary to take real measures for our defence. They were glad of this excuse.

June 16.

In the afternoon yesterday we were horrified at the number of big fires that broke out in so many different parts of the Tartar city, and when we saw that the Ch'ien Men Gate was blazing, and all the houses around in the same condition, we felt we were in great danger. If this got a hold, it would burn up the Legation district of

Peking very quickly. There are two parts of the city
—the northern Manchu city, containing the Imperial
palaces and garrison, also the foreign Legations ; and
the southern or Chinese city, containing the trading
population, theatres, and markets. Both parts are
joined in the form of the letter T, the leg or largest
part being the Manchu city on the north, with
walls 60 feet high, 40 feet wide at the top, loop-
holed parapets 3 feet high at the side, and square
bastions 100 yards apart on the outside face. At
wide intervals along the inside face are pairs of
inclined roads, 8 feet wide, for mounting the wall.
The total length of this rectangular wall on the
four sides of the Manchu city is about twelve
miles. Joined to this great wall on the south is
the much lower and weaker wall of the Chinese or
southern city. All nationalities sent men, even
these traitorous Pekingese, to aid us in extinguish-
ing the fire. The Imperial fire-brigade arrived with
great pomp, and could have furnished charming
costumes for some "extravaganza" in their get-up.
They had no idea how to put a fire out, but fortunately they had some hose, which, when used in the
telling places, proved most efficacious.

Our men fought this terrible fire side by side

To face page 26

FIGHTING THE FIRE 27

with the Chinese, and this goes to show how a common danger levels most things, even active hostilities. The Cossacks worked exceptionally well. This fire had been started by the rioters and thieves in the rich bazaar district of the city, under cover of which they hoped to get much rich booty. The wind being high, the flames gained great headway, and the tremendous Ch'ien Men Gate was soon ablaze. By eight o'clock the fire was somewhat controlled; but it burned all night, and when seen from the Great Wall it looked like a huge torch.

June 17.

Just one week ago to-day we got the telegram that the combined forces of England, the United States, France, Japan, etc., now at Taku, numbering 1,600 men and over, had practically seized a train at Tien-tsin, and, with workmen on board to mend the track where it had been derailed, had left at 10 a.m. to go to the relief of the Legations in Peking. Night and day, ever since that telegram came, we have been looking for them. The day after we received the news that they had started the Chinese cut the telegraph-wires, and so for one week we have been absolutely cut off from all communication.

No messenger has been able to get through the city gates, as they are carefully watched by the Chinese authorities, except—and I am proud of this — except that one old man whom Mr. Squiers had been good to (he used to be an old gardener of theirs) got through to Captain McCalla, who is with Admiral Seymour, and is in command of 100 men—Americans. The gardener had been able to deliver to him notes from Mr. Squiers, giving him most important information about ways and means to get into Peking in case they meet with opposition, and to bring back an answer, as well as other notes from commanders of other nationalities, to their respective Legations in Peking. From these letters we rather imagine that this " Tower of Babel" relief party does not agree as well as it might, but then, whoever expected a " Tower of Babel" to speak and work in unison ? Certainly never before the miracle !

So it is due to Mr. Squiers's personal management that we or any other nationality have heard anything from this party of 1,600 men, which undoubtedly must be but the beginning of large numbers of troops for what Lord Charles Beresford terms "the break-up of China." Our Legation, thanks entirely to Mr. Squiers's efforts, is the only one which has been in touch at all with the approaching column, and, by his minute instructions, when they get here they will be able to advance into the heart of our district—through the Water Gate—without having to take any of the city citadel gates. They say that in all crises, political or otherwise, some one man comes forward, takes the bull by the horns, so to speak, and does a man's work. Mr. Squiers, as far as all the Americans here feel, is *the* man in Peking.

The fighting, the weak and terrorized Government, the expected attack on the Legations, the horrible massacre of the Chinese Christians, the burning of all the missions, churches, and entire Christian communities, and last, but not least, the continued attempts—made, we think, principally by Boxers—to "burn the Legations out," all go to make these days very extraordinary ones.

Last night there was a scene enacted in our Republican compound that would be a fitting climax to any Bowery play where Jake, the villain, is finally run down. A regulation Boxer—red sash and all—was caught by a Russian sentry in the act of trying to set fire to the outhouses of this

Legation. He was assisted into the compound by the Cossack who discovered him, with no especial tenderness of manner, the Chinaman still clutching the picturesque and glowing torch with which the conflagration was to have been started. In three minutes coolies, soldiers, gorgeously dressed Legation servants, the European men in the compound, and we women, who were in the midst of our dinner, rushed out to see what it was (as we did fifty times a day, so far as that goes), to find this poor, writhing creature, who knew that he had nothing to expect but death in the next half-hour, as he had been caught red-handed. He was questioned, but to no purpose, and was then turned over to the Russians, as they had been responsible for his discovery ; and, although we all knew that that nation dislikes prisoners, we were hardly prepared for the bullet that, in less than ten minutes, whistled clear as a bell on the night air, and told us there was one Boxer the less in Peking.

Captain Myers has turned out to be a most competent officer, and the British Captain Strouts and the Russian Captain von Rahden have worked together splendidly for the object of saving our three Legations from attack and fire. These

BARRICADE BETWEEN THE AMERICAN AND RUSSIAN LEGATIONS

Copyright, M. S. Woodward

READING THE SENTENCE OF DEATH TO THE BOXERS CAUGHT IN THE RUSSIAN LEGATION

BRITISH LEGATION AND DEFENCE

Legations form a kind of triangle, our corner of which is the weakest owing to its bad shape. The British compound is excellent for defence, having strong, high walls, with stables or houses at the corners, one side having the canal running parallel to it, and the other having the Imperial carriage park.

When the time comes that the United States and Russian Legations can no longer hold out, the British Legation will be the stage for a terrible last act. So far, of course, things are not as bad as that, and fire is what we dread more than the disaffected Chinese soldiers or Boxers. Nevertheless, things got so critical the day before yesterday that food for a week for our entire Legation was sent over to the British compound, and each of us had sent over a dress suit-case with a change of linen, brushes, etc., so that in the event of our having to leave our Legation on the moment, we would not be absolutely comfortless and unprepared for a siege of several days until Seymour and McCalla could relieve us.

Yesterday things got so bad that our bugler played the "call to arms" four different times, which is the signal here for all women and children and all non-fighting men to appear at the big gate of the Legation, and within five minutes from that time Captain Myers will decide what must be done—whether the marines will escort us over to the Russian or the British Legation. After each of these alarms, however, it was decided not to send us quite yet. At the last alarm they kept us waiting, all huddled together like sheep, for an hour. And such an hour as it was—the constant reports of Mauser rifles, the absolute lack of knowing what was happening!

But at one moment I was obliged to forget the terror of it all and look at the humorous side. Mrs. Squiers was holding her youngest boy, a baby of four, in her arms, busy in quieting him. Her other boys, Bard and Herbert, were there, too, rather subdued, and last, but not least, our little cortège was completed by the arrival of the French and German governesses, each of them arguing violently in her respective mother-tongue. Mademoiselle is a large woman of ample proportions in wrong places, and she had her bosom filled with recommendation papers, which she fingered nervously —they were all she was saving in the way of valuables. Clara, the German governess, had forgotten

DIVISION OF FORCES

what her valuables were, and looked quite distraught with fear. She had a French clock in each hand, and was telling me in broken English, German, and Chinese how afraid and terrified she was. I said to her, "Gehen Sie mit mir," and she clutched my arm most painfully for the next half-hour.

As I have said, fifty men came to Peking from the *Newark* on May 31, and twenty of them with an officer were sent to defend the big Methodist mission near the Ha Ta Men Gate, which, because of its area and large stone church, is capable of a very good defence, and where all of the American Protestant missionaries that are lucky enough to be in Peking have gone. Much to Captain Myers' disgust—it is so hopeless to divide this small military force—the Minister insisted on sending this guard to them, instead of having them brought into our defended lines. Consequently, there is no officer to share the responsibility with him, or to give his men a sufficient number of hours off duty during the twenty-four. He himself gets about four hours sleep per diem, and that has to be taken in cat-naps and in a folding-chair. He is liable to have even that short period interrupted a dozen times by an over-anxious sergeant, who wakes him up to come and see this or hear that. He naturally feels the responsibility tremendously, and is on the *qui vive* at every shot. His men are in about the same condition. This strain has been without relief for eight days and nights.

Of the thirty marines here, ten, Dr. Lippitt tells me, should be on the sick-list, and imagine how they feel with a compound full of women to defend against perhaps thousands of half-crazed fanatics who at any moment may break into the Legation. Their work is splendid, and at all times they are prepared for the worst, but the constant strain is unimaginable.

Captain McCalla wrote in his letter, which Mr. Squiers's old messenger brought back to us, that he was in despair, as others in the relief party were not hustling enough. Our cry by night and day is, "When will the troops arrive?" Will they get here before or after some horrible massacre?

The men in the compound carry their rifles with them at all times, even when dining. Mr. Squiers a few days ago presented modern rifles with ammunition to all missionaries coming to the Legation. Taken collectively, these mission-

A RESCUE EXPEDITION

aries are a splendid lot of men, and are one and all most grateful to him for these arms, given them in this moment of awful danger to their converts, their families, and themselves. One night all left the table four times to run to the outposts, where shots and fighting were heard. In most cases, fortunately, they are not serious alarms —a few venturesome Boxers or Imperial soldiers running amuck in Peking after loot, who have decided to devil the foreigners. About three days ago we expected the troops any minute; now we are not so sanguine.

A detachment of men from the English Legation, our Legation, and the Russian Legation, started off under an English officer to rescue some of the thousands of Chinese Christians who are being burned and tortured by their enemies like rats in their holes. The tales that reached us through our servants, many of whom are Christian converts, and whose mothers, fathers, and wives are undergoing this continuous St. Bartholomew, made our men feel that we should try to do something for their rescue, even if we were not successful. Fortunately this party of men did not meet any large number of disciplined Chinese soldiers, finding them only in small groups. They killed a great many, and one could easily imagine how happy our men were to be able to kill these wretches in the very act of burning, looting, killing, or torturing. Sergeant Walker told me he had sent eight devils to glory; many of his shots he had seen take effect, and others he hoped had done as good work.

The "Nan-t'ang," a Roman Catholic church, founded in 1600 by the early Jesuit missionaries, was burnt by these Boxers, and as most of their converts and families live around the church, one can well imagine the slaughter that took place before it was finally fired. This is only one instance of the many missions and churches where the same kind of thing has happened. The Roman Catholics alone claim to have ten thousand converts in Peking.

The Pei-t'ang is a large fortress cathedral, and capable of splendid defence. It is the oldest and richest Roman Catholic stronghold. In its dual rôle of church and military position, which in the old days used to go hand in hand, this community reminds one of the wonderful and still extant example of feudal power, the Mont St. Michel

BOXER ATROCITIES

in Brittany, where cathedral and fortress dominate the higher part, and its villages cluster around the base. So here this Roman Catholic stronghold boasts the same arrangements, only with added hospitals and orphan quarters. It is a wonderful church to exist now, when the world is so old, and is supposed to be so peaceful. The French Minister has sent a guard with two officers to help Archbishop Favier, Superior of the Pei-t'ang.

In some instances hundreds of Christians thought it better to be roasted in their houses and burnt to death than to try and escape. Then, of course, the soldiers, Boxers, and thieves would loot the entire entourage of these burning communities, and, having once begun, they would not stop to inquire if the family were Buddhist or Christian. They were busy in this pleasant work when our posse of soldiers arrived on the scene of action, and the Chinese companies that had been detailed for this work were so disorganized by their lust of loot and cruelties that they were practically unable to attack us, and generally ran away, except in some rare instances, when they would rally and fight.

Mr. Pethick and Mr. Cheshire would raise their

voices in Chinese and tell the terrified people to come with them and they would be saved. Sometimes it was necessary to go into the houses to assure the people of this help. On entering the houses they saw many horrible sights—women and children whose lives it was too late to save. There was one small square compound that the Boxers had burned, while in the inside there was an entire family of Chinese Christians. The four walls were on fire, and these people were tied hand and foot. Our men were unable to save them in any way, and hastened to other places where they would not be too late. Babies were seen being torn in two. The result of this morning's work was the rescue of about one thousand Chinese Christians, who otherwise would certainly have been burned or killed within a few hours.

The officer in charge had them brought up Legation Street, which has lately been barricaded, and, except foreigners, no one is allowed to walk or pass. Two big barricades have been made at each end, one beyond the Dutch Legation, the other below the Italian Legation. And such a lot of poor, wretched people I hope never to see again. Half starved, covered with soot and ashes

THE RESCUED CHRISTIANS 39

from the fires, women carrying on their breasts horribly sick and diseased babies, and in one case a woman held a dead baby. One man of about fifty years old carried on his shoulders his old mother, who must have been every day of ninety years. She looked so withered and wrinkled, one had to think of the burning of Troy and Æneas. A great many of these people were terribly wounded—great spear-thrusts that made jagged wounds, scalp-cuts and gashes on the throat where the victim had been left for dead.

Dr. Lippitt, who came up with the marines, and the English and Russian surgeons set to work, and tried to patch these poor people together again, and they toiled, the three of them, steadily for many hours. I have never imagined that such stoicism as these wretched creatures exhibited could exist. They never uttered a cry or moved even when the surgeons were operating on them.

Then the question arose as to what should be done with them. They could not stay in the road; the Legations could not have them. Dr. Morrison and Dr. H. James hit upon one of the happiest of ideas—namely, the seizing of a lovely park belonging to a Prince Su, which runs parallel to the British

Legation, and is on the other side of the canal. It is so big there would be plenty of room for as many of these poor people as we shall be able to rescue, and being so near us, it will be quite possible for us to defend it. Dr. Morrison saw that the idea was carried out, and Dr. H. James went personally to Prince Su, and interpreted to him that it would not only be kind, but wise, for him to present his palace and park to his distressed fellow-citizens, who were being massacred by the Imperial soldiers in different parts of Peking, and in this way to furnish them with a refuge from the brutes who had killed thousands of them, and who were desirous of killing the rest. Dr. James implied that unless he voluntarily gave up his "fu" (meaning park), we would take it.

Prince Su was most suave, and said nothing would give him greater pleasure. There was probably some truth in what he said. He was only too glad to get as far away as possible from these Legation people, notwithstanding he would have to give up his palace. The danger for his life might be very great if he were suspected, even for a moment, of sympathizing with the foreigners, as might easily have been maintained by his enemies had he continued to live in this palace, which we told him he might do, as it was only his big park we wanted for the Christians. He vacated the same day, leaving all of his treasure and half of his harem. Thanks are due to Dr. Morrison.

How queerly things happen! These poor wretches, who had been tortured and hounded to death only two hours before by Imperial troops, were now housed in the palace of a mighty Prince, and almost within the shadow of the Empress-Dowager's palace. For three days this splendid work of rescuing has continued, but finally Captain Myers decided that, with all the night-watching and hard, long hours of sentry work, our men could no longer endure it. So it was discontinued, and I believe the other Legations have stopped for the same reason. The English, Russians, and our men usually went on these rescue parties together, and I never heard of friction, though they were sometimes under an officer of one nationality and the next day under another. The ten to twenty marines who were on these parties counted at a very low estimate that they must have killed 350 thieves, Boxers, and Imperial Chinese soldiers.

English Compound,
June 21.

Things are rapidly changing for the worse. On the afternoon of the 19th a communication came from the Yamen addressed to all the Ministers, saying that, as all, or most, of the European Powers had fired on the Taku Forts, war was practically declared, and, such being the case, they would be pleased for all the Legations to take their passports, and allow the Chinese Imperial troops to escort them safely to the coast, whence they could leave the country. This was a thunderbolt coming to the Ministers, and yet so plausible and possible did the proposition appear to Sir Claude Macdonald and Mr. Conger that they were almost ready to acquiesce if the Chinese promised proper transportation.

The German Minister, Von Ketteler, was very undecided—so much so that he determined to go by himself the next morning to the Tsung-li Yamen and have a quiet talk with the members, and in this way arrive at a conclusion as to whether there would be foul play in case we accepted their escort. As he had some knowledge of the Chinese language, he was able to probe a little deeper into a

PREPARING TO LEAVE 43

conversation than were his colleagues, who were naturally forced to speak entirely through an interpreter.

The majority of the Ministers—De Giers, Cologan, Knobel, Pichon, Salvago Raggi, etc.— were wavering, first to accept the proposition and then not to; but by five o'clock in the afternoon it was so generally believed that the Ministers as a body would accept the Tsung-li Yamen's ultimatum that all foreigners should leave the next morning at ten, that the executive members of the different Legation staffs had been out buying or procuring in any way possible large numbers of Chinese carts for the Legation personnel, and we women were packing the tiny amount of hand-luggage we were to be allowed to take with us, wondering whether to fill the small bag with a warm coat, to protect us on this indefinite journey to the coast, or to take six fresh blouses. Our hearts were wrung as to what to do, and while we were arranging and worrying about these trivial details the great diplomatic question was at a white-heat.

The Ministers were moving about from one Legation to another, arguing, talking — always talking. The strong men felt we must not leave

Peking until our own foreign soldiers arrived to escort us, but the weak men felt in despair as to which course to vote for. They did not like the idea of leaving either, but, oh dear, what a breach of diplomacy to receive their passports and then to decline to go! The strong, who knew, were so few, and the weak, who feared to disobey the Tsung-li Yamen, were so many, that it looked very much as if we were all to start out to our deaths the following morning.

During the afternoon two or three men made a visit to the Legations, hoping to be able to rally the Ministers into promising to cast an undiplomatic vote when the final conference should take place; and at one time Dr. Morrison took the floor, he being the spokesman for the vast crowd of intelligent individuals—engineers, bankers, trades-people, and missionaries—who one and all were in favour of waiting until Seymour and McCalla arrived. He looked the Ministers square in the eyes, and said:

"If you men vote to leave Peking to-morrow, the death of every man, woman, and child in this huge unprotected convoy will be on your heads, and your names will go through history and be known

THE TSUNG-LI YAMEN

MURDER OF VON KETTELER

for ever as the wickedest, weakest, and most pusillanimous cowards who ever lived."

On the evening of the 19th Von Ketteler sent an official letter to the Yamen, saying on the following morning, at ten o'clock, he should go to the Foreign Office, as he wished to discuss with the Tsung-li Yamen the trip to Tien-tsin, etc. A little before ten on the morning of the 20th he started to keep this appointment. He was in his official chair, his interpreter in one behind him, and both unarmed. Four of his Legation guard started out with him, but, after proceeding a short distance, Von Ketteler saw the congested condition of the streets and the great number of excited soldiers everywhere, and, rather than run the possibility of his men getting into a row, he sent them back to the Legation, and proceeded on his way to the Yamen in just such a style as a high Chinese mandarin would go through the streets, with only his two *maffus* riding on in front as outriders. These Chinese servants, being mounted, were the first people to bring the news back to the German Legation of his murder. Von Ketteler was passing a kind of guard-house where at all times a fairly large number of Imperial Chinese soldiers was kept. A number of them rushed out, surrounded his chair, and shot him many times in the back of the head. His interpreter was shot at as he was escaping with great difficulty, and a volley of shot was fired at him as he started to run. He escaped, however, to the big Methodist mission, where his wounds were dressed and he was cared for.

When the horrible news came to the German Legation, all the soldiers and officers there made a sortie as near as possible over the route taken by Von Ketteler; but it was not feasible for them to continue the search for his body, as they could very easily have been cut off from the Legation quarter by the Chinese troops, and have been placed in a desperate position.

When the story of Von Ketteler's murder had been confirmed, a shiver of horror shook each and every foreigner then in Peking; and we realized, perhaps for the first time, the horror of our position. Baroness von Ketteler, half crazed, wandered wildly about the most exposed and dangerous part of the German Legation. It was only by Lady Macdonald's telling her that probably her husband's body was at the British Legation that she was able to get her there, it being necessary, of course, for her to be put somewhere safe from bullet-fire, where women could be with her and do what little they could.

Those soldiers who killed Von Ketteler were Imperial Chinese troops, and represent the Empress-Dowager, and for them to have the audacity to kill a Minister shows us how much real power for the good there is in Peking to-day.

In the early afternoon the Ministers in conference decided that everyone must go to the British compound—that is to say, all women and children, missionaries, etc. The idea of getting our passports was no more discussed. Von Ketteler's murder had opened our eyes to our real position and the real attitude of the Imperial troops, so that the question of being escorted by them to the coast was never again seriously thought of for a moment, except to feel that Von Ketteler's death was the price we paid in order to learn of the positive treachery of the Chinese officials, although one must not forget there were many clever men in Peking who from the first argued in the strongest way against our going to Tien-tsin with a Chinese escort, begging the Ministers to wait until our own relief force, under Seymour, should arrive, and then let our own soldiers escort us to Tien-tsin. There is no question, however, that as a *body* the Ministers were for accepting the offer of the Chinese officials, and that it was only the tragedy of the 20th that made them see the impossibility of such a course.

The women and children and non-fighting men having gone to the British Legation, the men and marines in each Legation will stay and defend their respective fortresses as long as possible, and then make the English compound the one for a final stand. Legation Street, beginning with the Italian Legation, is completely cleared of all Chinese, and extends over the bridge up to our Legation, where we made big barricades, as we have this part of the street to defend; then the British Legation continues down from the bridge by the Imperial Wall up to the canal to the Tartar Wall. Besides this place of defence (which is the best position, and will be the final refuge for everyone), the Legations are defending themselves and their flags as long as they can; for, by keeping our lines as large as possible, when the end comes we shall be able slowly to retreat more and more, which will give us time, and by each day gained relief must be getting nearer.

As we have positive proof from the Chinese

MRS. SQUIERS'S GENEROSITY

that the Admirals have taken the Taku Forts, it must be that relief is very near, or they would never have jeopardized our lives in Peking by this overt act of war, unless at the same time they were in a position to save us in case the Chinese in Peking would retaliate by attempting to massacre us.

The American missionaries of several denominations, who have been defended in their big missions near the Ha Ta Men Gate by twenty of our marines, have been brought to our Legation to-day bag and baggage, not to mention babies. They consist of seventy-six adults and a large number of children, and while here Mrs. Squiers arranged a luncheon for everybody—men, women, and children; and, although she knows her food-supplies may possibly run short for her own large family, she opened her storeroom, containing staple groceries and many crates of condensed milk and cream, and urged these women to take, individually or collectively, literally as much as they could carry of the articles they most needed to tide them over until the troops arrive. These women had all had a taste of siege life, and already knew what it was to see their children show the lack of proper food;

and they consequently availed themselves fully of Mrs. Squiers's more than generous offer. It was a happy "mothers' congress" that denuded those storeroom shelves, and then this missionary convoy was taken over to the British Legation, and Lady Macdonald gave them the chapel for their lodging.

There are so many women in our United States Legation that the British have assigned us the doctor's bungalow. Dr. Poole is the compound surgeon, and we are living in comparative comfort compared to the people of other Legations. Politics seem to enter into the distribution of the Legation houses that are assigned to the heads of each Legation, and after a Minister is given one, he proceeds to arrange his people as comfortably as he can. Our house has not many rooms, but they are large, whereas the Russian Minister has been given the second secretary's house, which is in bad repair, and is anything but commodious. Sir R. Hart, as Chief of Customs, has one of the inferior houses, which is unfortunate, as his Customs officials are very numerous; but then, from time immemorial, the British Minister has never loved the Customs people's great power in having control of the huge revenues of China.

BARRICADE ACROSS THE CANAL TO THE FU

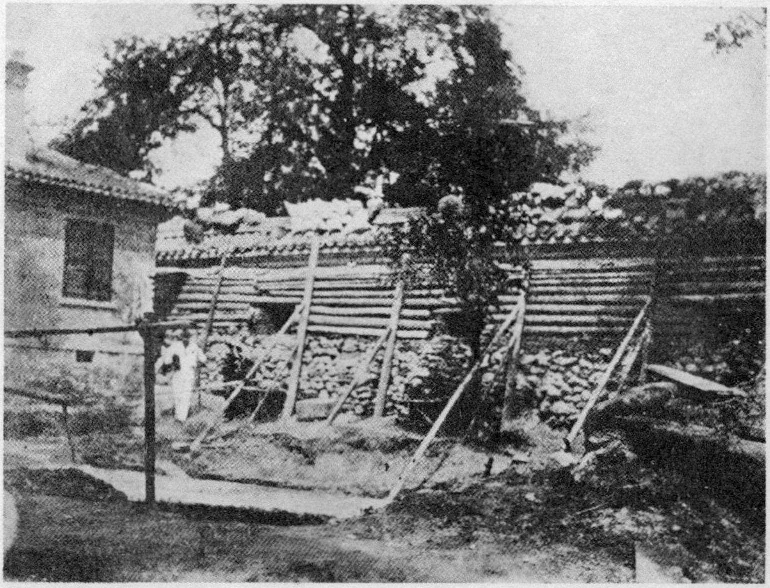

SANDBAG BARRICADE IN AMERICAN LEGATION

STILL WAITING FOR RELIEF 51

It is now almost two weeks since the troops started from Tien-tsin. Where are they? Seymour must be in command, and Sir Robert Hart suggests that, *when* he gets here, we call him Admiral See-no-more, or, if the Queen wishes to increase his rank for his rapid relief of Peking, she could with reason call him Lord Slow-come. The Russians themselves have christened Colonel Wogack Colonel Go-back.

Thank heavens that this compound is spacious— big trees and comparatively numerous houses. The Protestant missionaries are now all housed in the Legation chapel, where they have turned the vestry room into a model kitchen and the altar into a *table d'hôte*. A herd of sheep and a cow have been corralled and installed in the stables, so we shall have meat, in case we are besieged, for several weeks. But if we are not besieged so long, the most sanguine say that the Chinese, who are a nation of cowards, will get over their awe of the foreigner when they find how easily they have made him leave his Legations and collect in the strongest one. When the moment arrives when they entirely lose that awe, how easy it will be for Tung Fu-hsiang alone (even he controls about 10,000 troops around

Peking) to make a rush on us, although perhaps the only strength of his force lies in its numbers! To get in, to fire and massacre all the hated foreigners at one catch, is not at all impossible.

Legation Street being held by us Americans, we were allowed to have our trunks brought over here and placed in the five-room house which was turned over to Mr. Conger for himself and official family. Dr. Poole, to whom this bungalow belonged, ate at a mess, so that, not having any need for his stove in the kitchen of his house, it was immaterial to him whether it was broken or not, but what a difference it made to us! Mr. Conger's large family, increased by several guests from Chicago, had their meals cooked on this delightful stove at certain hours. Our family—that of the First Secretary of the Legation—is also very large, and accordingly we find it necessary to have meals at other hours; then, again, the Second Secretary, Mr. Bainbridge, arranges his *chow* at times during the day when it may be possible to cook something; and still again, Dr. Coltman, with his wife and six children, who have a room in the bungalow, have a definite time for their mess.

As we have come in so recently, our meals are

BOARD AND LODGING

mostly cold, in the spirit of catch as catch can. I find a great deal of coffee and tinned beef is devoured during the day with great gusto by our officers, soldiers, and civilians. Yesterday we brought all the tinned things over here from our Legation, but, as we are extremely uncertain as to the length of our siege, we realize it is just as well not to have too large appetites.

Mr. Squiers has been assigned two rooms of this house placed at the disposal of the United States Legation. They are situated at the back, opening directly on the filthy, dirty Chinese servants quarters. Mrs. Squiers, my maid, and I have the large room, which is practically the living-room for the family and mess of the First Secretary of the Legation. Our trunks, with two silver chests, and all the many dozens of tins of food that we brought from our Legation, are banked all round, up against the walls. The big double mattress on which we sleep is rolled up in the daytime, and we use it for seats as well as the trunks. We have no furniture, as Dr. Poole moved his bed to the hospital and found other places for the rest that he had, so the room is completely empty. Perhaps it is just as well, however, because we have great difficulty in finding a place big enough to spread our mattress out when night comes as our stores and trunks almost fill the room.

The three children have their respective cribs, which we were wise enough to bring over from our Legation. They are placed in the other room which looks out on the little avenue that runs through the compound. The air is much purer there than in our room, where we breathe the servants' air and gas which rises from a broken sewer. The French and German governesses are placed in the ends of small halls.

When we were collecting a few comforts— mattresses, cribs for the children, etc.—in our Legation to bring over to this compound, we carelessly brought, too, a light-blue satin eiderdown quilt, which we took from one of the bedrooms, and now we are glad to have it, for it serves as a most admirable portable bed. When his services are not needed as orderly to Captain Strouts, Fargo Squiers gets some hours of good rest on it. He takes it to any particular spot where he thinks his services may be needed during the night, and, with a childlike ability to sleep anywhere, and an old veteran's ability to wake up promptly, he finds

THE CHILDREN

this scrap of luxury from the old life doing excellent duty as a campaign adjunct. The sky-blue shade, however, is fast becoming a rich London smoke. Mr. Squiers, like other men who assist at the night-attacks, and must be ready to work anywhere at any time, sleeps in his clothes and his boots, usually in the American Legation, taking his rest in periods of forty winks at such time as he is not needed.

As things are not systematically arranged yet—in fact, we hope the troops will be here before we need to get things in such a condition—we do a good deal of cooking on our chafing-dish. When we turn the room into a nursery for the children (for we cannot keep them always in their own room, nor can we allow them to be much in the compound, as half the time it is thick with exploding bullets), it is then a sight to behold. There are a good many children here. Their one game seems to be "Boxers," and they copy in miniature what we grown-ups are playing in earnest. The younger ones are forced into being the attacking Chinese, and I am afraid when the big ones repulse them, they occasionally get very real bumps on their heads. They have small sandbags and barricades, and their Chinese war-whoop of *Sha, sha!* (Kill, kill!) is a creditable imitation of the real thing. It is all very clever, and they are all very full of life, and I help them to play, for it's a good thing that they don't realize what all this may mean, and we hope that relief will come before they lose their spirit and before they know.

One can see, on walking about, missionary children, of whom there are quantities, elbowing Ministers Plenipotentiary, and the latter going about without collars. The Belgian Minister, for instance, is a good example of the condition of to-day. He, with his First Secretary of Legation, M. Merghelynckem, Chevalier de Melotte, and his English valet, have been most gallantly defending their Legation for a long time without help of any kind. They killed many Boxers who attacked them, but they were so few that they found it impossible, after eight days, to hold out any longer, and were forced to leave. A party of Austrian soldiers went to their rescue and escorted them into the Legation lines, as the Belgian is quite distant from this centre. They had the pleasure of seeing their compound fired fifteen minutes after they left, and knew it was being looted as well. They then became "refugee colleagues," and stopped first with the

THE MISSIONARIES' WORK 57

Austrians, then came here. They have for wardrobes the clothes they have on their backs, only M. Joostens has one extra blue cotton shirt and one piqué cravat.

Our Protestant missionaries are working steadily and continually wherever it is most essential, and besides doing everywhere the work of men, they have taken under their wing the care and feeding of that vast number of rescued Chinese converts who are now in Prince Su's park. Most of the Roman Catholic brothers, in contrast, not only do not raise a finger to work, but in no way occupy themselves usefully.

Firing seems to continue at all times, but it is mostly over our heads. Yesterday Boxers tried to loot and fire the Dutch Legation, which is next to ours, and Captain Myers turned our machine-gun on the crowd for a minute and killed six Boxers, so the attempt to loot was not successful, but the burning of the compound continues. The Methodist Mission, so lately vacated, was looted and burned last night. So much happens in every twenty-four hours I can hardly keep account of it all, and as a background to the hourly horrors that develop is the continuous snipe, snipe, sniping, mostly by our own men, who are on roofs of buildings shooting at the constantly approaching incendiaries.

All food-supplies which can be procured in any way from anywhere by anyone have now to be turned in to the committee in charge of food, and everything is deposited with them on the erstwhile tennis-court of the British Legation, which is their headquarters. In fact, everything of a useful nature is stored there, whence it will later be distributed where most needed. The two foreign shops in Peking are Imbeck's and Kieruff's, and as they are too far up Legation Street to be defended in any way, they have been abandoned by their owners with their contents. The committee on food-supplies, although greatly desiring the stores on the shelves of these shops, would not attempt to get them, as anyone making the attempt would become a perfect target for Boxer snipers as soon as he left the protection of our last barricade on Legation Street.

Imagine our surprise when, late in the afternoon, a Chinese cart, driven by Fargo Squiers, a boy of fifteen years old, came thundering into the British compound with the upper part of the cart riddled with bullet-holes. He was heading for the two

A PLUCKY ENTERPRISE

rooms in Dr. Poole's house which had been allotted to his family, and his freight consisted of dozens of tins of the above-mentioned supplies from Imbeck's death-surrounded shop, which he had procured at the greatest risk to his own life. The committee were about to order him to unload his desirable cargo with them, to be used for the good of the public, but upon hearing that the boy had ridden into the very jaws of death to procure these supplies, and had dared what no man in the compound had dared to do, they told him he could have the disposition of them, for by his rash valour he had well earned the lot.

It seems he procured a Chinese cart and forced two coolies to go with him. On their way to Imbeck's one was killed by a bullet in his head, and though the other survived to help him load the cart, after arriving in the courtyard of the place, he had difficult work, as coolie number two tried to run away, and twice the boy had to point the muzzle of his rifle at him, indicating what he would do if he made any further attempts. They were fairly free from shots while actually loading the cart. On the return trip every yard of the way they were peppered by bullets, and the second coolie was wounded, but not killed. This boy saw what he thought he ought to do, and he did it; but what a terrible price might have been paid for these stores! Apropos of stores, these last certainly are welcome. Our mess is large, and so many tins were given to the missionaries and other needy people before we came to the British compound that we would have felt the lack of staple groceries tremendously had not this large windfall arrived.

The committee on food supplies have two articles in tremendous quantities—all kinds of tobacco (long black cigars and Egyptian cigarettes) and dozens of cases of wines, mostly red and white, which will be a great help to the Continentals here. These supplies were procured by the committee from deserted shops near enough to the Legation centre to make their procuring not too dangerous. I think the general public was more pleased at the arrival of these stores than were the missionaries in charge, for with misgivings the question arose surely in their minds, Were these things sent to us from Heaven or from the other place?

Friday, June 23.

The excitement to-day is terrible, and much more intense than anything we have yet had. Fires

FIRE AND LOOTING

are starting in all our "lines." The horror and dislike of leaving our respective Legations to concentrate in the British is nothing compared to the fact that if we leave our Legation the Boxers and Chinese soldiers will immediately burn them and loot them, and this may give them such a lust for loot and pillage that it may become an incentive strong enough to overcome their national fear of attacking, and make it most terribly difficult for us to hold out until the troops come. Until the troops come! What a wail that is! and it is heard at all times, and all people take their turn in asking somebody else, "When will they come?"

This afternoon we were in Mrs. Coltman's room, and her sweet baby was asleep in a funny, old-fashioned, high-backed crib. Although the sound of exploding bullets was to be heard outside the house, we were much startled to feel one—you can't see them, they come so fast—enter the room, hit the headpiece of the baby's crib, detaching it from the main part, and bury itself in the opposite wall. An inch lower and it would have cut through the baby's brain. His mother picked him up, and all of us flew into a room on the other side of the house, where we felt we would be free from shot, at any rate coming from that direction.

We were accompanied by the wife of the Chief, Mrs. Conger, conspicuous for her concise manner, and an open follower of Mrs. Eddy. She earnestly assured us that it was ourselves, and not the times, which were troublous and out of tune, and insisted that while there was an appearance of warlike hostilities, it was really in our own brains. Going further, she assured us that there was no bullet entering the room; it was again but our receptive minds which falsely lead us to believe such to be the case. With these calming (!) admonitions she retired, and I can honestly say that we were more surprised by her extraordinary statement than we were by the very material bullet which had driven us from the room.

All women are busy sewing up sandbags to strengthen our defence, while bullets are raining into the compound like hailstones. A man comes rushing to where we are working, and tells whoever is in charge of filling the sandbags that a hundred, or as many as possible, must be taken to such and such a barricade, or it *cannot hold out*. We get snatches of the real state of affairs very often in this way.

AUSTRIAN LEGATION ABANDONED 63

June 23.

Yesterday, the 22nd, the Austrian marines vacated their Legation, although Von Rostand, the Austrian Chargé d'Affaires, and other people greatly criticized them for having left too soon. These marines then went to the French Legation, and M. and Mme. von Rostand became Lady Macdonald's guests at the British Legation. The Belgians stayed with the Austrians until they left, when they came to this compound, and the Belgian Minister also became a guest at the Legation. The Dutch compound and the Austrian compound are still burning.

Yesterday at ten o'clock in the morning a sort of terror, almost unaccountable, seemed to sweep over the entire length and breadth of our lines; the French soldiers got in a terrible funk, left their Legation to Boxers, fire, or anything else that might appear, and ran all the way without stopping to the British Legation, where they said everything was "lost." The Germans also got the fright, but after coming up Legation Street half-way, they turned back, and not only took a stand in their own Legation again, but they sent men into the deserted French Legation and kept it manned, so that if the

Boxers came they would be resisted, and not be allowed quietly to take possession.

The Russian compound is the only passage-way by which the American marines can escape and retire to the British Legation, and it was understood that in case of an attack from the Chinese serious enough to necessitate everyone leaving their Legations, the Russians would not close their big gate opening on Legation Street until our American soldiers had entered, when they would hold out there (in the Russian compound) as long as possible, and then retreat all together to the British Legation. Our Russian friends, however, forgot this little arrangement, and when our men were also seized with this panic and left the Wall, and retreated through our Legation across Legation Street to the Russian gate, they found it not only locked and barred against them, but no one near enough even to hear them knocking. They excused themselves afterward by saying they had left a tiny gate open farther down the street, but as none of our people knew there was such an entrance, we thought this a rather poor excuse.

However, in an hour's time, after this terror had passed over the entire line, our marines had returned

FRENCH AND GERMANS

to the United States Legation, and had manned the Wall again. The French returned later to their Legation which the Germans had kindly guarded for them in the interim, rather disheartened to think that the scare they had started should prove to have been only in their own overwrought minds. As the French and German Legations occupy two important positions, and are constantly being attacked by Boxers and soldiers, the French Legation could have been taken very easily by the Chinese had the Germans not occupied both Legations. They are directly opposite each other in Legation Street.

Our men already have the reputation of being the crack shots of any of the guards in Peking. It has been noticed that when our men aim they bring down their game—whether the game is a Chinese soldier's head or a Boxer.

Yesterday it seemed too hard that, after the nervous excitement and fright to everyone in the morning, Providence did not withhold the terrible fire that broke out almost in our very midst in the park directly next the Wall. Each hour seemed more terrible than the one before. A huge column of smoke went up into the air, and in its centre forked tongues of flame burst out. It seemed impossible that this enormous fire—one so large or so near I have never before seen in my life—would not in an hour or so completely burn us up. The Boxers or soldiers who had so successfully started it must have been overjoyed to see their work, knowing it would take almost superhuman power to put it out, although I am sure they could not have thought it possible that we could extinguish it.

There was little enough hope written on people's faces in our compound to make us feel, for a time at least, that perhaps the Chinese might be successful, and by burning one wall that played so important a part in our defence, they could enter and massacre us without having to attempt an attack by scaling. Had there been a wind blowing this enormous column of fire in our direction, we could not have fought it at all, and the entire long wall which divides the British Legation from the Empress-Dowager's carriage park would have fallen.

Our men scaled ladders and worked like New York firemen in the way they strove together and in the good sense they exhibited. I suppose man is able to keep his head clear when he knows that this may be his last chance in this world to save

QUENCHING THE FIRE

his skin from Chinese savages, and that his arm
develops in consequence a good deal of strength.
Men who were on top of the wall, throwing down
buckets of water on the fire, and handling with as
much care as possible the small rubber pipe that
we are using as a hose, came down every fifteen
minutes, to be relieved by others, for they were
half scorched, some badly burned from cinders and
falling débris, and all of them had lost their breath
in that terrible heat.

It must be remembered that while these men
were on this wall they were beautiful targets for
Chinese sharp-shooters, and we found afterwards
there were many in the Chinese troops. There
were three wells in the compound, and from the two
biggest there was a line of men and women passing
buckets, ewers, and any other kind of vessel that
was available, filled with water, to the men who
were actually fighting the fire on the wall. One
realizes the heroism it takes to continue working
at a fire though half scorched, but what shall one
say of these men who worked under the ordinary
danger of a scorching fire, and who knew they were
the target for the continuous rifle-fire and sniping
that was kept up throughout? The sky was grey,

and the men on the Wall made agonizingly big and black silhouettes for the Chinese to aim at.

If I live to be a thousand, I could never see a queerer collection of people working together to extinguish a fire, and with the object to save themselves from a massacre—coolies, missionaries, soldiers, and Ministers Plenipotentiary working and straining every muscle for the same object. Surely Peking never before saw such unanimity of her foreign residents. I was in that line of men and women passing buckets, and so was the wife of the French Minister, and many other well-known women.

Fargo Squiers, Dr. Martin, and Dr. Poole, surgeon for the British Legation, were three soot-covered people who came to our rooms after the fire was entirely out,—which meant they had worked desperately for many hours without stopping. To say they were thirsty would not be truthful—they were parched. Dr. Poole whispered that the only cup he knew big enough to quench his thirst was a big loving-cup that was in a small closet in a corner of the room (this house having been his before the siege), and that if I would fill it with Apollinaris he would put in the whisky.

MRS. R. S. HOOKER

To face page 68

I filled my order, and he poured out about four fingers of Scotch into the bottom of that big loving-cup, and as he drank it slowly, holding it by both hands, I thought I had never seen such thankful eyes as were his during that long and pleasant well-earned drink.

Again to-day thousands of sandbags have been made by the women. Shooting continues all the time, and to-day a cannon was fired from the Ch'ien Men Gate, which we hope may mean that our troops are coming and the Chinese resisting them. Prince Ching is supposed to have under his command in China fifty thousand troops, and he must be friendly to us, or we feel he would have ordered half of his troops to Peking before this to finish us. It is stated that some of them have shot at the Boxers, but this is hardly credible. Prince Ching is a Prince of the first Order, and head of the Tsung-li Yamen. Dr. Morrison is the most attractive at our impromptu mess; he works wherever a strong man is needed, and he is as dirty, happy, and healthy a hero as one could find anywhere.

June 24.

Two weeks ago to-day the troops started from Tien-tsin. Yesterday by 11.30 a.m. the Hanlin

Library, directly behind Sir Claude's house in the compound, was fired by the Chinese, and the way we fought the flames I described yesterday, only perhaps the men felt a little stronger. They have succeeded once in putting out an enormous fire, so why should they not be able to do so to-day? This time, however, the wind was against us, so that from the morning until seven o'clock at night we were fighting it desperately.

How absurd it is to have any "consideration" for people like the Chinese! After the big and dangerous fire of the day before yesterday, the committee on fortifications and defences suggested that the world-famous Chinese College (the Hanlin Library) should be burnt by us in such a way that the Chinese could not use it as a position to fire on us from. There was danger, too, that they would fire it themselves, taking it for granted that the fire would surely spread to such an extent—aided by themselves with kerosene—as to burn this entire end of the Legation. The Defence Committee was afraid of this, and at a conference of the Ministers it was discussed, and more or less unanimously disapproved of. "Such vandalism!" they said. "This trouble will soon be over, and then what

THE HANLIN LIBRARY

a disgrace to have to acknowledge to the world that we deliberately burnt one of the finest, if not the finest, libraries in the East!" We only had to wait twenty-four hours to see that our consideration for the famous library was thoroughly thrown away, for, notwithstanding the troubles " will be over in a few days," the Chinese seem so anxious to destroy us before these troubles have passed that they themselves burned this gorgeous old library, containing as it did all their oldest and most revered literature, *in the hope* that they could burn out a large enough part of our Wall to facilitate their getting in.

The great danger was over by seven o'clock, but careful sentries watched all night in case a strong wind should start, and small isolated buildings were burning all night, so that, looking down from our house to that end of the compound, it made one think of the blazing flames one sees at night in the oil districts of Pennsylvania. With these terrible fires the Chinese are clever enough to keep up a volley of rifle-fire, so our labour is a frightful danger to every man working. The suspense was hard to bear, because it was over five hours before the most optimistic dared say, " We are comparatively out of danger;" and nobody knew just what would happen if this end of the compound was to go, for this British compound is looked upon by all as the strongest and last resort in Peking, and that is why, of course, all of the women and children and stores of every description have already been sent here.

Twenty-five Chinese Sisters, who were rescued from the Nan-t'ang, come to our tiny little courtyard at the back of our house—on which charming view, by the way, our windows look—and cook in a big caldron their portion of rice that is allowed them by the General Committee. These people and all of the families of Mrs. Coltman's "boys," and Mrs. Squiers's "boys," fill up our tiny backyard with their cooking, etc., until, from the propinquity of these people, one is almost convinced that one is living and sleeping in the heart of the Chinese settlement of San Francisco.

The marines at our Legation, who naturally will not come here until they are forced to, are in a very bad way about food. From May 29, when they arrived in Peking, they were fed by a Chinaman who contracted to feed them all at so much per man, and he fed them splendidly, but since we have been besieged he naturally has no market to call upon. Mr. Squiers has fed them for some days out of his own storeroom, but each meal makes a terrific hole in his supplies. There are fifty men and two officers, and naturally they do not get satisfied on one tin of sardines and a loaf of bread. We have cooked rice in great quantities, putting many tins of corned beef into it, cooking it in the same big caldron that the Sisters use. Preparing the food over here makes it very difficult getting it to them, as there is constant sniping going on, and it is extremely dangerous to walk from one Legation to another.

June 25.

So far the moral of the Legation, or, I should say, of this compound, is decidedly good. The weather is very warm, but the heavy rains that generally come at this time of summer are not here yet. Only a few babies are sick with dysentery, and there are some cases of scarlet fever and malignant malaria. The hospital, a house of four rooms, only holds a comparatively small number of patients. Let us pray it will not have time to fill up. Dr. Velde, a surgeon of the German army, who has been detailed for three years to the Legation in Peking, is a man who for very clever and consecutive work has already been decorated by his Emperor. His forte is surgery, and it looks as if he would save the medical day here in Peking. Dr. Poole, I think, will consult and work with him. One of our marines has already been killed, and two are at the hospital wounded. These people, who are the first to lose their lives and get hurt, make one feel that truly this is war.

I was at the hospital with Mrs. Squiers this morning. Several men were brought in, and they all had to wait their turn to be operated on, and the two nurses were so busy assisting with the work in connection with the operation of the moment that nothing was done for a wounded Cossack who was laid on the floor. He was covered with blood, and it trickled down his chest and formed into a pool all around him, his face an olive-green—the colour one sees in unskilfully painted pictures of death— so livid, I never believed even dying people could look that way. He lay there for some time, everyone in authority too busy except to tell me to do what I could for him, and keep the flies from bothering him until he should die, probably in twenty minutes. He was shot through the lungs.

People continue to be cheerful, but it is strange

considering that we have death around us morning, noon, and night. The gossip, if one can so call the reports and rumours that are circulating throughout the compound nearly every few hours, is that a Russian declares he knows their troops are coming, because during the night a sentry saw a green rocket go up into the sky. It is supposed that the Chinese have no green rockets; therefore, as the Russians constantly use green rockets, it *must* be a signal from the Russian troops to let us know they are practically at the door. And so on and so forth.

To-day Dr. Morrison went over to the Fu, where the Chinese Christians are, to assist Colonel Shiba in some difficult and dangerous barricading work, and incidentally to take a part in a sortie. He was in command of a squad of Japanese and Italian soldiers, the latter most ineffective, and the former magnificent. They cleared the Chinese out of some alleys which Colonel Shiba decided must be added to their lines for the protection of the Chinese converts. The brunt of the fighting fell on the Japanese, and one was killed and three wounded. Such a clever idea it was of Dr. Morrison's and Dr. H. James's to put these poor wretches in Prince Su's park, which, owing to its close proximity to the Japanese Legation, seems now to fall upon the Japanese to defend.

Dr. H. James met with such a terrible end yesterday! From the gate of the British Legation facing the canal, he looked down towards the Imperial Wall, and seeing there several Chinese officers carrying a regimental flag with which he was familiar, he started out, as if on the impulse of the moment, to parley with them. He was watched with breathless interest. Although from the time he left our wall until he reached them he held his hands up to show he was unarmed, they grasped him in the fiercest way, dragging him over the bridge beyond our range of vision. The horror of his too probable fate is hanging like a pall over the compound. We cannot understand how a man, knowing the Chinese as well as he does, could have been so mistaken in their character as to trust himself to them with such confidence.

During the two fires in the Mongolian Market Place and in the Hanlin University a great many Chinese were shot by us, and when possible we straightway threw their bodies into the flames. Unfortunately, some Boxers were captured during the almost hand-to-hand fighting that has taken place, and confined in this compound. They were all shot at dawn this morning.

Captain Myers has been in command for two days and two nights on the Tartar Wall, with no sleep. This afternoon the marine quarters in the United States Legation caught fire and for a time it looked as if the whole American compound would go, but with hard fighting it was put out.

Mr. Cheshire, of the United States Legation, is willing to take the most difficult and dangerous work wherever an interpreter is needed, and for some nights now he has been on the Tartar Wall directing and encouraging the picked Chinamen forming the gang of labourers who nightly help our marines to strengthen the barricades. Many Chinamen who advance towards our lines too rashly, are killed every night, and after hours of this work the number of corpses that accumulate is astounding. For the sake of the health of the community, Mr. Cheshire has to spend much of his time superintending his gangs in throwing dead bodies over the Wall, and to-day he facetiously remarked he thought he should be dubbed Major-General of the Corpses, as he comes in touch with so many. Such gruesome tales as these do we hear and talk of daily!

June 26.

Yesterday afternoon, at four, five gorgeously costumed Imperial Standard bearers appeared on the bridge in Legation Street with a flag of truce, saying the Emperor would send later a despatch to the bridge for us to read, and that there was in consequence an armistice. It was brought later, and it read: "The Emperor desires the Ministers to be protected. Therefore, firing must cease, and a despatch will be handed to them later on the bridge." It was apparently not brought; but on seeing some mounted Chinese officers belonging to Jung Lu's regiment passing over the Imperial bridge, we hailed them with a white flag, and with some soldiers to back up the meaning of the flag, we spoke to them long enough to find that they were going the rounds of this part of the town, telling their people not to shoot this night on us, as there was an armistice. We told them to send the Emperor's letter or despatch (which has not yet arrived on the bridge) to the British Legation. They promised that it should be brought to us, but it has not yet arrived at noon to-day.

Last night I was talking to M. Pichon, the French Minister, when the French Interpreter of

HOW LONG CAN WE LAST? 79

Legation came up to us in great excitement, saying the Russian officers had heard, without any possible doubt, *les sonneries du canon* of the Russian troops. It is in this way we hear so many tales that one is lost when one tries to think. The captains of all nationalities have had a council of war, and they agree that with great care and hard work we can hold our own for eight or ten days longer, but after that we are lost.

Mrs. Coltman, the mother of six lovely children, was speaking of the impossibilities of clean linen or having any washing done. "But after all," she said, "what does it matter? If the troops come within ten days, my children can wear what they are wearing; if Peking is not relieved within that time, we will all be dead." She was not melodramatic, but spoke very quietly. A hundred other remarks of this sort that one hears daily go to show how the people really feel about our condition. Women with husbands and children suffer horribly. They dread lest their children may die of disease or by torture, as certainly would be the case if the Chinese get in—as they are notoriously cruel and without mercy even to babies—and fear for their husbands, who may be killed during any attack.

At one o'clock this morning a terrific firing began, apparently coming from all sides at once, which proved to be the case later, when the officers in charge of the defence compared notes. At this Legation the air hummed with bullets, but the noise was so frightful one could not tell if all the Legations were being attacked or just the British. They tried to frighten us, and they certainly succeeded with women, children, and some men, but, thank heavens, the officers in charge of defending us and the sentries—most of them, at least—know that our high walls and strong barricades are our safety, and that, unless good and well-aimed artillery is brought to shell them down, with our soldiers and soldier-sailors to man them, it will be hard for the Chinese to get over the Wall and end our lives.

It all seems like a story from the Middle Ages to be able to place such confidence in the strength and manning of our walls. Certainly the foreign-drilled Chinese soldiers must be down at Tien-tsin, and we are owing our present immunity from properly aimed artillery-fire to the fact that the Chinese gunners here are utterly incompetent.

After this fiendish attack had been in progress long enough for everyone to get up and dress,

A QUESTION OF DRESSING

Mrs. Conger came back to our room, and her manner was more than tragic when she saw me lying on my mattress on the floor, not even beginning to dress for what I suppose half of the women in the compound believed to be the beginning of the final fight. She said: "Do you wish to be found undressed when the end comes?" It flashed through my mind that it made very little difference whether I was massacred in a pink silk dressing-gown, that I had hanging over the back of a chair. or whether I was in a golf skirt and shirt waist that I was in the habit of wearing during the day hours of this charming picnic. So I told her that for some nights I had dressed myself and sat on the edge of the mattress wishing I was lying down again, only to be told, when daylight came, that the attack was over, when it was invariably too late for anything like sleep (which way of living is distinctly trying), and after a week of it, when one has so much to do in the day hours, I had come to the conclusion that, as it was absolutely of no benefit to anyone my being dressed during these attacks, I was going to stay in bed unless something terrible happened, when I should don my dressing-gown and, with a pink bow of ribbon at my throat, await my massacre.

This way of looking, or I should rather say of speaking, did not appeal to the Minister's wife, but I must say that at such terrible moments during the siege it is a great comfort to be frivolous. By making believe that one is not afraid one really lessens one's own fear. "Assume a virtue if you have it not," says our beloved Shakespeare. After Mrs. Conger's visit on this same terrible, ear-deafening night came Clara, Mrs. Squiers's German nursery governess, and she needed all sorts of assurances to convince her that a massacre was not in progress at that very moment.

These attacks are very terrifying, and to talk to a person two feet away one has to shriek. People one sees are either apparently most optimistic or desperately pessimistic, nothing between. It is a horrid thing to see big, strong men unable to hide their innate cowardliness, and shirking all duty of the slightest personal danger.

Friday, June 29.

One or two days have passed without my opening my diary, but they are very much like the days that I have already written about. The weather is very warm, but all able-bodied men are working desperately hard over trenches, bomb-proofs and

VAIN RUMOURS

barricades, or putting out more fires that have started at different places. Several attacks are constantly being made in opposite parts of our lines, with perhaps one big general attack in the afternoon and one during the night, which causes great excitement and sometimes great fear in everybody's heart. Then comes more excitement when the rumour arrives that a big fire is breaking out in the French and American Legations, or we hear that someone, who has just come from one of these Legations, says that he has heard the officer say they probably cannot hold out much longer, with fire to fight as well as the Chinese, and in ten minutes the report is all over the compound that these Legations have been abandoned, and half of the soldiers defending them killed. Such a quantity of rumours that are circulating every day, only to be denied and proved untrue an hour later! It is incredible!

In the case of the Legations who are still holding their own, it is very hard on the women whose husbands are still staying with the soldiers until they finally evacuate. These poor women naturally wonder, " What is my husband doing? Is he dead, and when they evacuate will he be amongst the lucky number to retire to the British compound alive?"

Hard work is kept up on the important barricades, and men do hours and hours of manual labour. The women make thousands of sandbags daily, and help at the hospital, and make short rations go as far and look as attractive as possible under the circumstances. The only strong men in the compound who have no special work to do are Ministers Plenipotentiary. There is no head-work to be done now, and some of them don't take kindly to physical work.

The British Legation Library is a complete one, and occasionally some inquisitive soul will go to it and try to find, compared with other sieges and massacres, what place this one will have in history. The nearest similar harrowing siege seems to be that of Lucknow, where a heterogeneous multitude, closed up in the Residency, were holding out against fearful odds in expectation of relief by Havelock's Highlanders, resolved to die of starvation rather than surrender, for in surrendering the fate of Cawnpore awaited them; and in thinking of these things we recollect that the Tartar rulers of China are of the same tribal family as the Great

TARTAR AND MANCHU

Mogul, who was the head of the Indian Sepoy Mutiny. But the King of Delhi was trying to regain his throne, whereas the Empress Dowager has no such excuse in making war on practically all the nations of the civilized world.

The Tartars and Manchus are an alien race, although the rulers of China for many centuries, and have always been inimical to everything which tends to increase the power of foreigners; whereas the Chinese are cleverer, from being so constantly in contact with Europeans on the sea-coast, or anywhere where they can find gain or advantage in trading with them, and have become, compared, at least, to the ruling Manchus in Peking, progressive and modern. The Emperor and his party for progress were completely snowed under in 1898 by the Empress-Dowager and her old Manchu Conservatives, who, lacking the desire to accept anything modern—even diplomatic relations of the most simple kind—decided, in a childlike and unreasoning rage, that everything foreign must be swept down into the sea, and it really looks now as if the first steps of her policy may be realized.

Lady Macdonald has forty Europeans in all to feed three times a day including servants, and at table they sit down thirty-three. She is very sensible, and has only one dish. Nobody thinks of dressing for dinner, except the Marquis Salvago, and I think it shows things are truly far gone when English people dine, but do not dress.

Our little mess is very attractive, and as our stores are much more numerous and of a greater variety than those of almost any mess here, we manage to have, up to the present at least, a most satisfactory one. We have tinned beef as our *pièce de résistance*, and rice is our mainstay—of a necessity, as it is that of which we have most. Tomato catsup tastes very good in this hot weather. Oatmeal is another staple that we have, and as luxuries we have a good stock of jams, tinned fruits, tinned vegetables, sardines, tinned mackerel, Liebig's extract, a big box of Stilton cheese, coffee, tinned butter, and white flour. Mr. Squiers has a large supply of champagne, and every night we have one or two quarts with our siege dinner. The men work so hard, and the women's nerves are so much on edge, that a small amount of stimulants is surely a blessed help.

Our mess being comparatively small, these delicacies are lasting nicely, as we use them with

A BLESSED ICE-BOX

discretion, for we remember in the old days before the siege a dollar was a dollar, and would buy a tin, but in these days a tin has no market value—they cannot be bought. When one's tins are gone one can eat horse-meat and rice. We brought a small lead-lined ice-box with us from our Legation, which seemed foolish at the time, but which is a great comfort to us now. We keep our wine and drinking-water in it, and also well-water, which is very cool, so that our drink is somewhat cooled, and is not the same temperature as the air. No other mess can attempt to have things cool, and this is one of the features of our room— that we are as comfortable as we can be under these extraordinary circumstances. During this sizzling weather cool water is a great comfort. It is so hot that a tin of meat, if left open all night, spoils by morning.

There is an English newspaper-man, who, when he can spare a few moments from the siege-work, gets his camera and takes a few photographs of things as they are. He is fond of chaffing, and to-day the Committee on Fortifications are of opinion that the house used by the French Minister, M. Pichon, is being undermined by the Chinese from outside, though indistinct noises, etc., are as yet the only proof of it. The Minister was more than usually perturbed about this new personal danger, and was not pleased, or at all amused, at the remarks addressed him. "I am making photographs for the Paris *Figaro* of this siege. Very soon your quarters will be blown up by dynamite. My camera is ready to take the photographs, and as you will be the principal person in it, how would you prefer me to take you—as your Excellency is going up wholesale, or as you are coming down retail?"

At this time people are not well-balanced, it seems to me. Some take the daily horrors as a matter of course, are more callous than they should be, and the others are so miserably pessimistic and mournful that one shuns them, fearing to catch this infection. There is a young man here who has been known to indulge in temporary aberrations, usually at night, following long, hard days of work in the broiling sun. On one occasion he was on his sentry beat, and on being relieved by his chief, the sight of whom was too much for him after having walked some hours on his dangerous sentry route (which seemed doubly dangerous in

A NARROW ESCAPE

the pitch-black night) he, doubtless brooding over his probable approaching death, pointed the muzzle of his gun straight at his relief. "C'est à cause de vous, misérable, que je suis venu à Pékin et encore c'est à cause de vous que ces belles années de ma jeunesse seront salement terminées ici!" By not moving an inch the man thus threatened undoubtedly saved his life, and most intelligently agreed with his attacker, "Probably so; let's talk it over." In a few minutes the crisis had passed, but the following day the man who had been in such danger requested the General Committee to change his night sentry duty to a different part of the compound, so that his young secretary should not again be tempted to hold him responsible.

Sunday, July 1.

I have been quite under the weather, to use a civilized expression, and I assure you that things have got (not are getting) to such a state that to live and act and talk as one would do at home is quite out of place. How soon people get accustomed to an idea! Now that we have prepared our minds for a possible massacre we seem to be getting back, to some degree at least, our old spirits. Now that

I am well, how much nearer seem the soldiers who are coming to relieve us!

What a place this compound would be for an epidemic! There are barely enough mattresses for the wounded and dying at the hospital, so that, should we have one, and take a house for those taken sick, I am sure that there would be no ordinary comforts of any kind for them; they could only be isolated. Let us pray that we will have no such horror to add to the already long list.

The hospital is already full, men lying on straw bags in halls—crowded in every conceivable corner. They are brought in dying and wounded every day. Dysentery has its grip on almost everybody here. The treatment is almost to stop eating and to drink rice-water in large quantities. Our four-times-divided cook—the other three messes in the United States bungalow have a lien on him too—is off for some hours daily on work which all personal servants have to give to the General Committee. When the kitchen is comparatively free, Mrs. Squiers, my maid, and I make gallons of rice-water, thick, nutritious but tasteless, which we bottle in quart-bottles and place to cool in our zinc-lined, cold-water-filled box. It is placed in a corner

THE PEKING SMELL 91

of our two-roomed quarters, and the constant stream of men coming and going to that box would lead an uninitiated observer to believe that at least a Hoffman House bar was hidden there and doing a steady business.

The rainy season and the bad time of the year *par excellence* has begun, and the temperature is like a Turkish bath without the clean smell. Apropos of smell, a whole story-book could be written about the Peking smell. The dry heat was nothing compared with this damp temperature, that seems to soak out of Mother Earth the most incredibly disgusting odours. There are so many dead dogs, horses, and Chinese lying in heaps all around the defended lines, but too far for us to bury or burn them. The contamination of the air is something almost overpowering. All men who smoke have a cigar in their mouths from morning until night as a protection from this unseen horror, and even the women, principally Italians and Russians, find relief in the constant smoking of cigarettes.

On the 29th Dr. Lippitt, who came up from Taku with our marines, was sitting in front of the Minister's house smoking a cigarette, when a bullet struck a limb of a tree near by, and, glancing down, struck him in the thigh, fracturing the bone. He is most dangerously ill, and we shall not know for several days whether he will have to have his leg amputated or not. He is an attractive man and a thorough Virginian. We used to play tennis with him and Captain Myers before the times got so terribly out of joint.

To-day the Germans were driven off the Tartar Wall close to their Legation, which caused a great deal of excitement. They were driven off by Chinese soldiers, some of whom were Tung Fu-hsiang's men, and others were Prince Ching's especial troops, which seems queer, as we have supposed all along that Prince Ching was friendly.

The Germans could see from the Wall that the Ha Ta Men Gate is being strengthened, and people who know say that the troops who are closing the gates in such a warlike way are doing it as much against the violent and uncontrolled soldiers of Tu Fu-hsiang, who are notorious for the manner in which they loot and murder, as against the allied Powers. They say that all Chinese families in Peking who have anything to lose have left the capital, as they realize that if the foreign troops

A PANIC ON THE WALL

come there will be great looting, and if the Chinese troops are successful there will be looting and worse. Mr. Pethick tells me that during the Japan-China War, when it was considered highly probable that the Japanese would march on to the capital, thousands of Mandarins and people of wealth left Peking with their families and with as much treasure as they could carry. It is natural to suppose that the same fright exists to-day.

This morning our men, the Germans following, retired in a panic from their barricades on the Wall to the United States Legation, momentarily expecting to see Chinese hordes occupy the German position and theirs. After an hour's wait they retook the Wall. This example, however, was not followed by the Germans. During this hour the excitement was intense in the British compound. The report that the Wall had been evacuated caused a panic, for this abandonment of the Wall would enable the Chinese to mount their guns on this portion of it, directly commanding the British Legation, and to fire down on us, and no one can say how long we could hold out against such an attack. In such an event we will put women and children into deep bomb-proofs that have been made for that purpose, which are covered with logs, sandbags, and dirt, and are shell-proof. These trenches we have made as near as possible like those used in the siege of Ladysmith.

As the Germans have been unable to regain their positions on the Wall, the difficulty for Uncle Sam's men has been increased fifty per cent., as they must now be prepared at all times, either during the day or night, for an attack by Chinese from both directions. This sentence, "to give up the Wall," could be, translated into siege language, "the beginning of the end," and this news was most terrifying to us. I think that there are few who in their heart of hearts have given up hope of the troops coming soon. Nevertheless, the facts remain that if we cannot hold the place it would not take very long for us to be annihilated, and if the troops come a day after we are finished, a miss is as good as a mile, and we don't care then when they come. If we had not had the greatest luck in the world we could never have held out like this to the present date, and what the Powers can be thinking about not to send a column to our immediate relief, knowing, as they must, that we could never hold out against artillery, is beyond the reasoning power of the people in this Legation.

Are the allied Powers fighting each other, or are they fighting their way up here?

Yesterday an unsuccessful sortie was made by Colonel Shiba from the Fu to capture a gun, and six men were killed. These offensive measures seem to gain us nothing, and we always lose men.

Apropos of Colonel Shiba, he is a splendid, small person. He has taken his position here by the strength of his intelligence and good right arm, solely because the Ministers and the guard captains were not especially inclined at the first morning conference to listen to him—in fact, I don't know that he tried to talk, but it is all changed now. He has done so splendidly in his active and continuous fighting in the Fu, and has proved himself such a general, that his opinion and help are asked by all the commanders. His men are all so patient and untiring in their long, long hours behind the barricades, and are so game, in great contrast to the Italians who are with him defending the Fu. One can only hope for Italy's sake that her soldiers in Peking are the worst she has.

Now that we have got down to the primitive *motif* of all nationalities fighting for their lives, the racial friendships and animosities are very obvious.

The British and American are almost one people here; although the expressions, "D—— Yankees!" and "D—— lime-juicers!" are interchanged, they are used in a spirit of affection. The dislike of the Russians for the British is so cordial that it is only equalled by the feeling the British entertain toward them. The frankness of this avowed enmity is delightful. Our compound joins the Russians, and they love us and we love them in as strong a fashion as they hate their English neighbours on their other side. Baron Von Rahden orders his men to work and fight as much as possible side by side with our marines, as in this way he hopes to increase the efficiency of his untrained guard. These men can't speak the others' language, but are the best of friends. The Russians are all called "Rouskies" by our guard.

The Germans are somewhat by themselves, and fraternize with no one. Their Legation is at one end of the defended lines, and opposite the French. They are full of sullen rage at the unavenged death of their Minister, and when they are fighting or defending barricades in conjunction with other nationalities, and perhaps under command of an American or British officer, they have become notorious for their utter disregard of ordinary military precaution and unnecessary daredevil recklessness. The French are also far from the base of the defended area, and come in for attacks. They are assisted by the Austrian guard, some Belgians, some Customs students and unattached Continentals who are able to use a gun. The Customs students constitute a splendid force of young men, but as they are of all nationalities, they are apt, in taking their active fighting positions, to gravitate to the guards of their respective countries, although in many instances they simply join the weakest spot. The Japanese are defending the Fu with the greatest valour, and, needless to say, are tremendously pro-English and anti-Russian.

We now feel that our tactics must be entirely defensive. Although to-day is Sunday, most of the women in the compound, missionary women included, are working hard at sewing sandbags, the non-fighting men filling them. Beautiful material of all kinds is being used for these bags. Liberty satin curtains from London and linen monogrammed sheets from Paris are cut up ruthlessly to be used. One hundred thousand bags, as near as they can be counted, have been made already. It was principally in the Fu, defended by gallant Colonel Shiba, that the materials procured were so gorgeous. Bags were made from the bolts and rolls of brocades and satins that constituted part of the treasure left by Prince Su in his palace when he so kindly turned it over to his persecuted fellow-citizens. This is the one bright, wonderful bit of colouring in the compound : it is the barricades of thousands of big sandbags made entirely of these gorgeous-coloured satin brocades—sky-blues, blood-red, Imperial yellows— thousands and thousands piled one upon the other. It has been built from the ground up to the second story of the Chancery building—a rather high house for Peking. It was made at this building, as the firing has been very heavy here—a most extraordinary, butterfly-coloured barricade; and if it were anywhere in the world except in this siege in Peking, there would be seen lines of artists, with sketch-book and easel, trying to put this unusual effect on canvas.

Tuesday, July 3.

For several days past the Chinese on the Tartar Wall have been bolder and bolder, and yesterday

THE CHINESE DRAWING IN

they built their last barricade so near ours that they could, and did, throw big rocks over into our lines, which, by a lucky chance, hurt no one. The moral effect of this dangerous propinquity was terrible on our men. They felt that there was only one almost ineffective barricade between them and hordes of Tu Fu hsiang's soldiers—the notoriously cruel Mohammedan chief and his bandits. Mr. Squiers was the first to appreciate this great danger, and certainly the first to think of the cure, and, what was more to the point, he put it through. The pros and cons were discussed with Sir Claude in conference, and it was decided that a charge down the Wall must be made, and soon, or else we must leave it entirely, and that none of the Americans were willing to do, as we had been there from the beginning, and although the Germans gave up their position on the Wall, we were not content to do the same.

Captain Myers was more than ready to lead the charge, and he was given twenty British marines, fifteen Russians, and thirty of our own men. At dawn this morning, about three o'clock, he charged the Wall. No one in the compound had gone to bed ; the excitement was very great. We sent sixty of our fighting men on this sortie, and if they failed we should have lost what we could ill afford to lose. We felt that the odds were about even, and *that* waiting at the hour of dawn was frightful. The charge was successful, and two Chinese regimental flags were captured. Sixty-five dead Chinese soldiers were afterwards found between the two barricades, but the actual number killed and wounded is unknown. Our men came back at five o'clock carrying their dead and wounded. This has been the only effectual offensive measure accomplished during the siege. Captain Myers led it most gallantly—an inspiration to his men—and was wounded by a spear-thrust in the leg.

Thursday, July 5.

The Glorious Fourth came in during the last twenty-four hours, and the Chinese kindly announced the fact about 3 o'clock a.m. by a violent firing from all sides, which terrified everybody, but like most of the similar attempts recently made, only resulted in giving everyone a bad fright, and materially weakening some one or two points of our defence. Von Below, of the German Legation, notwithstanding his military physique, seems to be

CAPTAIN JOHN T. MYERS

To face page 100

MUSIC AND MASSACRE

developing into a man of moods instead of a man of action, and the story comes over from his quarters that during this last terrifying attack he was seized with the premonition that this was the end. He preferred to meet his doom by making his piano interpret his last feeling. The music from the "Valkyrie" that he drew from that instrument was marvellous. He played, regardless of time and place, in a soul agony, but was rudely awakened some hours later to be told that the attack was all over, and that for this time at least he was not to be massacred in a storm of music.

To-day the moral atmosphere seems worse. I think that it is because absolutely nothing has reached us from the outside world to let us know that our respective Governments care what becomes of us. My personal attitude, compared with my co-besieged friends, is one of extraordinary cheerfulness, simply because, perhaps owing to my youth and health, I can feel no terrible fear for the future, but, on the contrary, am distinctly hopeful.

All the hope that has been caused by seeing nightly green lights that look like search-lights is falling very low, because they have not got nearer at all, which would not be the case were they signals used by our approaching troops. Where can the troops be? Are all the Governments so gullible as to believe the Chinese Ministers in their different countries, who are probably assuring them of our safety, or can they be so criminally selfish as to be fighting diplomatically among themselves as to what each Power shall have in the way of future sharing of China after our rescue?

The consensus of opinion among the Ministers here is that the different nations will agree to allow the Japanese or the Russians, who control large fighting forces within a week's march of Peking, to send a relief column to Peking with the sole object of relieving their eleven Ministers Plenipotentiary, exacting a promise that on this expedition there should be no *coup d'état* or punitive measures, but simply relief of their distressed representatives. Weeks ago we were told to come to the British compound for a day or two, but as yet there is not a sign of help. Every day deaths occur of our best fighting men and officers, and the question is, with men going in this painfully regular way, how long can we hold out? Soon women and children will constitute the only forces of the compound. The deaths each day are fortunately small in number, but a great many are wounded, some very badly, which make them as good as dead as far as fighting goes. The Russian officer in command says that we cannot hold out longer than for one week at the most, but more sanguine people say that, with good luck, three weeks can be tided over.

Captain Myers's wound of his spear-thrust is not as slight as was expected, and he has much fever. It was very sad to-day to see the funeral of another baby. The second funeral of the day was one of the most popular and attractive of the Customs students. He was shot through the liver while cutting down a tree near the Hanlin Library, and died two hours later.

Fifty men are in the hospital, twelve have been killed, and there are a few convalescents walking about the compound. We did not say so at the time, but we can say now, thank Heaven! the Chinese have tried to fire us on all sides, so that in this way there are very few places or houses where the Chinese, who are sniping at near range, can secure cover. By means of terrific efforts, in which everybody joined, to extinguish the fires, serious harm was averted, although our enormous wall, giving on to the Mongolian Market Place, had a breach in it that took a great deal of hard work on the part of the men to rebuild, or, I should say, to mend, with rocks and sandbags, in such a way as to make it safe.

These rocks were moved with great difficulty; they had been in place so long forming the pavements in this compound. How fortunate, from a defensive standpoint, that when we came here we were allowed some servants, our coolies included! Most of these are Christians, because the Buddha men as a rule deserted when they saw how things were going; and now these servants are put in gangs, all of them having to work for the common need in building barricades, filling the thousands of sandbags to strengthen the defences, and doing necessary sanitary work, also at times working shoulder to shoulder with our soldiers when a barricade caves in from the enemy's heavy fire. One barricade, for instance, was destroyed by the Chinese. The coolies, working with the soldiers, rebuilt it, though exposed to a galling fire from Tu Fu-hsiang's men all the time. One afternoon six coolies were killed.

These men, whom we call by the general term

OLIPHANT'S FUNERAL

of "coolie," classing them thus for convenience, are often scholars, being teachers of Chinese to the missionaries or interpreters, and yet they work without complaint in the gangs, though they are in every way unaccustomed to manual labour.

At four o'clock we had another funeral, for Oliphant, who was shot. I was present, and the English chaplain, Mr. Norris, gave us a short service. It was very sad to see his body, wrapped only in a piece of sacking, let down into the ground. The grey sky, occasional bullets flying over our heads, and a few claps of thunder, with flashes of lightning, made a fitting background for the burial of this lovable young man. His brother, a great tall, gaunt fellow, looked his part in the most pitiful way as chief mourner. Before we leave Peking many will be the Chinamen who will be killed without quarter by the Customs students in revenge for the untimely death of their comrade. All the Ministers Plenipotentiary were there, and poor Sir Robert Hart looked weak and haggard from deep grief at the loss of his favourite subordinate. Oliphant was buried only three hours after his death. We have no way of keeping the dead for a greater length of time.

Horse is the principal article of diet. Several days after we arrived here the beef was eaten up, and there remained but a small flock of sheep, which fortunately was brought here while there was time. There are 1,293 Europeans to feed daily in this compound, and rice is the dish *par excellence* for everyone. Mutton, however, is distributed to the sick, women and children, to the extent of a quarter of a pound apiece every third day. There are a lot of horses, ponies, and mules in the compound which we have kept alive by feeding with straw, and every day two animals have been slaughtered and distributed among the messes. Then the coolies have a kitchen, where they can come whenever their work makes it possible, and they get rice and horse-meat. It is queer to see how many people acknowledge that they like it, having eaten it now for two weeks. Of course, a great deal depends upon the animal, but they agree that mule and pony are better than horse. Some people even who have among their stores plenty of canned or tinned beef prefer the fresh horse-meat. At our mess, however, we have a prejudice against it, and as long as we continue to have the tinned beef we will not send for our share of the animal.

The May races having come off before the siege, most of the diplomats had not disposed of their horses and polo ponies, and the all-important question now is not if "Cochon" will win more cups in future, but if his steaks will be tender. Things are so queer now. The one cow which still gives a small amount of milk, needless to say, has not been killed for her beef, but is carefully tended for her baby-saving fluid. The president of the largest and most influential bank in Peking, besieged here with us, has received a wound which absolutely incapacitates him for active work. He can only hobble around on a crutch. He has volunteered to tend "Miss Cow" and assist her to find the few blades of grass which are still to be had.

I went with an officer to the Hanlin Library, where the sniping is still constant, but not quite as severe as it was, owing to the good barricades with which we have strengthened the position. The Chinese fired this wonderful library of Peking so ruthlessly that nothing is left there but thousands of charred and burnt books, and some evidences of the charming courtyard and grass plot where the old Chinese savants used to go and read the ancient manuscripts in Sanskrit and other dead languages. Here I found the bank president, a great power in China in ordinary times, quietly tending the cow, watching her from an antique stone bench. Surely the shade of some ancient philosopher must be shocked into asking himself, " And what have we here ?"

The Customs mess at Sir Robert Hart's has an invariable menu. At breakfast, rice, tea, and jam ; at tiffin, rice and horse ; at dinner, rice, horse, and jam. We have splendid stores—better than any in the compound—so we live better than any mess here. We have quite a supply of Bishop's wonderful preserved California fruits, not very sweet, which are most delicious during this hot weather, because they do not make one thirsty ; then we have macaroni and tinned tomatoes. We make our corned beef into croquettes sometimes, but generally have it put into a curry with rice. Yesterday we had a great treat for dinner. Our cook, who is an enterprising and daring soul, went outside of our lines into the Mongol markets at great risk to his life from snipers or being

OUR MESS AND MENU

waylaid by the enemy, and procured one dozen tiny chickens. Sir Robert Hart came to our party.

Menu.

	Remarks.
Celery bouillon	Liebig extract, celery.
Anchovy on toast ...	Anchovy paste.
Broiled chicken	Procured at risk of cook's life.
Green peas, fried potatoes	Tinned peas and two potatoes.
Bean salad	Tinned beans.
Black coffee	Plenty of coffee.

The chickens remaining from the cook's raid are being kept in a basket and fed as if they were babies, and will be used entirely for the children. We count eight at our mess as regular members, but our guests are constant and numerous. Its personnel consists of Dr. Velde (who does such glorious surgical work), Dr. Morrison, Mr. Cheshire, Mr. Pethick, Mr. Squiers, Fargo Squiers (who is Captain Strouts' orderly), Mrs. Squiers (who, because of the great generosity in freely supplying from her limited stores those who are in need, has been called by many in this compound the " Lady Bountiful "), the three children and two governesses, and myself. We usually have missionaries in to tiffin, and our more intimate friends, many of whom are sadly in need of food, to breakfast and dinner.

The Russian Legation is so situated that at one point their defence is very weak, and they have almost nightly attacks at such close quarters with the Chinese, that the fighting is sometimes hand to hand. The men of the Russian guard were undrilled sailors, who had been forcibly enlisted from inland villages in Russia, and Von Rahden, their commander, and his under-officer, to keep them from running away when these close-range fights begin, get behind them and stick them with the ends of bayonets, so that they in turn will advance on the Chinese with fury. He claims that this is the only way to teach undisciplined troops to advance at close quarters, as they always become seized with terror—and I don't wonder a bit, for the Chinese in attacking blow on shrill horns, shriek, howl, dance with the wildness of dervishes, and advance with the cruelty and cunning of Indians.

Von Rahden is frequently up all night, and when he is, he usually comes to us for breakfast, which we have at any time between 6.30 and 8 o'clock. I have especial charge of the coffee-pot, and when the members of our mess have been up all night on

MRS. SQUIERS

To face page 110

BREAKFAST DIFFICULTIES

duty, they look as if they could drink it all, instead of the one cup I have to limit them to. What a difference, instead of having your maid bring your breakfast-tray in the morning when you ring for it, to be waked up from a heavy morning nap at six o'clock by knocking on the door, to find two or three powder-begrimed members of your mess humbly inquiring: "How soon will breakfast be ready?" They have probably been up all night on the firing-line, and are dog-tired and faint.

We tell them to come back in half an hour, and then our skirmish begins. The sleepy cook is routed out of the Chinese-filled courtyard under our windows, and told it is time to cook the wheatena, the coffee and soda-raised biscuits, for which purpose he repairs to the broken stove in the box-like kitchen. We take a hasty sponge-bath, and our rough-dried shirt-waists and golf-skirts are donned, and we are ready for the day. Next we roll up our straw mattress, place it in a corner, and put the small eight-sided Chinese table in the middle of the room. We boast four chairs, and as our mess ranges from eight to twelve people, the ones who come late sit on the silver trunks or on the floor.

A fresh table-napkin we have procured from somewhere, and on the table we place some green leaves for decoration, and breakfast is announced. Besides Von Rahden, another breakfast guest we have almost daily is the Rev. Mr. Gamewell, a missionary who appears the mildest of men, but who is developing into one of the strongest in Peking. He is the brains of the Defence and Fortification Committee. Before entering the ministry he was a star student at Cornell, in the engineering department; and now this entire compound and the outer lines are included in his hands, and his recommendation for barricades, countermining to protect against the Chinese undermining, of which we are constantly aware, are all carried out as near as possible from his orders. Before dawn he is at work to take advantage of these hours of comparative quiet, to see just where the weak spots are, and how he can best provide for their strengthening during the coming day. He is a stooping figure, very quiet, and rarely speaks to us, and, when he does speak, never about what he is doing. He told me his working hours are so continuous, and everybody calling for him from every quarter, that he did not believe he could keep on if it were not for the hour's rest and good hot breakfast that he gets daily in Mrs. Squiers's rooms.

Another member of the mess is Dr. Velde, the German surgeon, who is doing such wonderful and constant work at the hospital day and night. He performs unheard-of operations one after another, and on the same old kitchen table that we found for him. The antique rifles used so frequently by the Chinese inflict the most heart-rending wounds, the treatment of which, to be successful, surely calls for surgical genius, and, thank Heaven! Velde has that. He is short, thick-set, and blond, with stumpy little hands and a keen blue eye, and is wonderfully practical and matter-of-fact. The various messes near the hospital asked him to join them, but without affectation—he knows he is the only surgeon in Peking, and he must guard his health—he answered: " No, I go only where I get the best and the most food;" and having been asked by Mr. Squiers to come to us, he gladly accepted, while reiterating the same reason for joining us that he had given for refusing the others. His duties are so constant that he usually is only able to get in to breakfast and dinner.

Another feature of this siege is one which shows what marvellous executive ability some people have. The proprietor of the Peking Hotel is Chamot, a Swiss who has played a wonderful part in the drama of our imprisonment. There have naturally been numbers of people without stores of any kind, and people who, if they had stores, would have no place to cook them; so Chamot stepped forward and undertook to feed daily I don't know how many people. When we were first assembled in the British compound the confusion was something terrific, and he gave food to all those who had nothing, and later he made a permanent business arrangement to provide food for those who had no means of messing themselves. Among these are many Roman Catholic priests and twenty-five Roman Catholic Sisters, saved by himself and his wife from the Nan-t'ang just before it was burned, besides numerous families and detached individuals having no stores, who would have had a most serious time without his assistance.

These Sisters were fed by Mrs. Squiers for many days before Chamot volunteered their care. Of course, the variety that he supplies is not wonderful, but he gives them horse-meat, rice, occasionally some tinned vegetables, and a kind of coarse brown bread, made from an inferior flour, which he bakes himself. For so many people it is quite marvellous how he feeds them so regularly. He has a few coolies to help him at his hotel, which is near the French Legation, and there he personally superintends the cooking of the two messes, one at twelve and one at six o'clock, and brings it up in a Chinese cart to the British compound, always at the risk of his own life from snipers. One cannot but wonder how long he will be able to continue his good work. Chamot's Hotel in Peking is known in the siege vernacular as the Swiss Legation.

Monday, July 9.

A day or two ago an old-fashioned cannon was found in a shop near Legation Street, where they made Chinese stoves—a kind of foundry. It is undoubtedly one of the guns brought up to Peking by the English and French in 1860. Mr. Squiers promptly took a great interest in this ancient piece of ordnance, hoping that we might make some use of it. He, with Mitchell, a gunner's mate from the *Newark*, have worked assiduously in their efforts to clean off the rust of forty years and get it ready for use. During the cleaning process they made projectiles of bags of nails. They took the "International," as the gun was christened, over to the Fu and fired the bags of nails at a Chinese barricade, thus serving the double purpose of cleaning the gun and causing some damage and immense fright to the enemy. The noise of the explosion was so much greater than anything the Chinese had heard coming from our lines that five sentries incautiously put their heads above the Imperial Wall to ascertain what was going on, and were promptly shot down by our guards. Some Russian ammunition is here, intended for a gun which should have been forwarded from Tien-tsin at the same time as the ammunition, but which, most unfortunately, Colonel Wogack failed to have put on the last train, and we find it can be fired from the "International."

To-day a European boy died of dysentery. Last night the "International" was taken over to the Hanlin, where it was used to great advantage in breaking up a barricade that the Chinese had made, and which they have been strengthening daily for their convenience and protection while engaged in the pleasant occupation of sniping our men. The

LOADING THE "INTERNATIONAL"

Copyright, M. S. Woodward

AMERICAN AND RUSSIAN MARINES AT WORK ON THE BARRICADE.
BARON VON RAHDEN ON THE RIGHT

day before yesterday Von Rostand, Austrian Chargé d'Affaires, was shot at the French Legation—where, I understand, the rifle-firing and shelling is terrific —somewhere near the eye, and they fear he may lose it. His wife is nursing him there. M. Merghelynckem, the First Secretary of the Belgian Legation, killed two Chinese yesterday, and in killing one he undoubtedly saved the life of the French commanding officer. He does good work, and is a fine shot, but is erratic to a degree, and I don't believe he loves his English colleagues as much as he might. He left yesterday for the French Legation to take up his abode there, where he surely will be treated with great consideration, having saved the life of their officer, although there he is given eight hours of sentry duty, while here he had but six hours.

The other day he brought me five long Chinamen's queues, which he had cut off the heads of Boxers he had killed, as a souvenir of a day's work. It means to some Chinese—the cutting-off of the queue—a great and unholy mutilation, and these trophies hanging up in our living-room for a few days were obviously things of terror to our Chinese servants, although they had been cut from the heads of their dread enemies, and we soon disposed of them. Yesterday the Austrian commanding officer was killed, shot through the heart. At first we kept a record of the dead or badly wounded men as they would be brought into the hospital, but now they come in so often that we cease to note the exact number.

People—the sanguine ones—say that it is quite likely and reasonable that help will not come for a week or two, and in this way, if the troops do not come, they can say, with childish satisfaction, " Oh, I never expected them before." When we first got here all the Ministers and everyone said: " Certainly by the first of July at the latest." Now they are actually saying: " Certainly by the first of August "!

Yesterday—Sunday—there was a lot of good work done. Nevertheless, Mr. Norris, the chaplain, who is one of the hard-working members of the Committee on Fortifications, gave us half an hour for the service held in Lady Macdonald's dining-room—the regular chapel of the compound being occupied by the American Protestant missionaries—and I must say that it was comforting. This room is something of a wreck, denuded of all draperies for sandbags, walls riddled with large and small bullet-holes, a life-sized painting of Queen Victoria occupying the entire wall at one end of the room, hung quite crooked and peppered with shot. A great beam from the ceiling protruded some 4 or 5 feet down into the room, where it had been forced by a spent cannon-ball crashing into the side of the house, and over all this ruin was the unmistakable atmosphere which clings to a room where many people eat three times a day, and where the staff of servants is not equal to the work. It was but six weeks ago that I was a guest at a most charming dinner given in this very room, surrounded by what then seemed to be the unutterable and interminable calm that comes from the possession of the best things to make life pleasant in the Far East. The other denominations had their services as well some time during the day.

The hot weather began last week, and the thermometer is 109° in the shade. I wear shirt-waists and short skirts; the men wear filthy clothes that they work in and most of them sleep in. They never wear collars—no washing of linen for three weeks, and, from the looks of them, most of them only shave every fourth or fifth day. Life is now settling down to a routine, and one would think that the people of this compound had never done anything else all their lives but get up during each night when a general attack begins. Each man goes to his appointed post, or if for a change we have no general attack, the men quietly get up at all hours and go to their sentry work.

The Marquis Salvago sits chatting with his wife, a very beautiful woman, in a *chaise longue* most of his time. M. Pichon, the French Minister, nervously and ceaselessly walks about, telling every one who chats with him: " La situation est excessivement grave; nous allons tous mourir ce soir." M. de Giers, the Russian Minister, walks eternally between his Legation and the British compound, and looks every inch a Minister. Poor Señor Cologan, the Spanish Minister, and doyen of the corps, is very ill. M. Knobel, the Dutch Minister, offered his services as a sentry to the Committee on Defences, but stated at the same time that he did not know how to shoot, and was very short-sighted. Needless to say, his offer was not accepted. Mr. Conger, the American Minister, walks about. Sir Claude Macdonald, the British

Photo, Elliott & Fry

SIR CLAUDE MACDONALD

To face page 120

Minister, is now the Commander-in-Chief, unanimously elected to that position by his colleagues, and he tries sincerely to do his duty as such. I believe he is fully competent, as he used to be a captain in the British army before entering the diplomatic service. His path is a thorny one, however; most of the Legations are so jealous of this compound being the centre and last stronghold *par excellence*, that they are outrageously inconsiderate of all orders issued, and, notwithstanding the great gravity of the situation, they put everything in Sir Claude's way to keep his plans from reaching successful maturity. A small incident may be cited to show this horrid and prevalent spirit.

The French had put in an application with the Committee on Fortifications for picks and shovels to be sent to their Legation for important night barricade work. The missionary in charge of them at the British Legation failed to send them; either they were all in use on equally important work, or there was an oversight on his part. Having failed to receive them, Herr Von Rostand, the Austrian Chargé, who has joined the French in their compound, at twelve o'clock last night returned to the British Legation, where he and his wife were accepting Lady Macdonald's hospitality, and took it upon himself to wake Sir Claude up, and insultingly shouted that Sir Claude was responsible, and he alone responsible; that the French Legation was not being properly defended, etc. (especially the etc.). Sir Claude said that he would discuss anything relative to the safety of the Legations at any time in the proper manner, but the way that Von Rostand spoke made it impossible for him to talk to him at all. The Von Rostands then took up their abode at the French Legation, which was natural more or less, as the Austrian soldiers are helping them.

A question going round the compound is: When the French and German Legations must be given up, where will the Von Rostands go? The fact that one is a Minister or Chargé does not help to find one new quarters, as every room, hall-way, and closet, was long ago appropriated. The charming doyen of the Corps Diplomatique, the Spanish Minister, Señor Cologan, sleeps on a mattress in the tiny hall of the house that was given to the French Minister for himself and official family. He has to go to bed late and get up early because people have to walk over him. He has a tiny shelf on

RAIN AND DISCOMFORT

which to put his few toilet possessions, but he sleeps in all his clothes, as everyone sees him. The Dutch Minister sleeps in a tiny storeroom of the very small Second Secretary's house, that we now call the Russian Legation, where the fifty-one people composing M. de Giers's official personnel are housed. As this room is a storeroom, his nights are a constant fight with cockroaches. Such is the way rank is treated when it is a fight for life.

July 16.

A steady rain has begun that promises to last for several days, a sure but not very heavy downpour, and with it comes a greater number of mosquitoes and fleas than would otherwise be the case. The sticky black flies seem to be of a different family from those one is accustomed to elsewhere. It is awful to see them feasting themselves on these filthy and ill-smelling Chinese people, half of whose bodies are usually covered with a hundred of these pests; but the Chinese are so accustomed to them that when they prepare their food they do not object if some, or I should say a great many, get into it. The "slaughter-house," of course, is a great centre for these disgusting flies, and as we are only a few doors from it, the feeling of having these beasts swarming over everything in one's room, oneself included, is distinctly unpleasant. To an imaginative person, who may have been so unfortunate as to study " The Life of the Microbe," these scavenger flies would certainly cause him to lose his mind.

The room at the back of Dr. Poole's house, which we occupy, is damp, and all night the fleas and cockroaches that appear would horrify anyone. We sent our mosquito-nets and hair-mattresses to the hospital, so that every night we lie on our straw-stuffed bag, doing duty as a mattress, on the floor, and unless one lies in a pool of bug-powder there is no such thing as sound sleep. Until quite recently we had no insect-powder, and the nights were unimaginable. Our bodies were most frightfully bitten. Lately, however, a steward at the hospital concocted a powder of materials which he had on hand. It makes one sneeze, it is so powerful ; but under these circumstances sneezing is a joy. One knows our arch-enemies are dying, although this does not affect the ungetatable mosquito, who sings on nightly.

Last night young Warren, of the Customs, was carried through the compound on the way to the

hospital, his face almost entirely shot off. I knew
him quite well—had danced with him often; he
was a charming fellow. He died at daybreak this
morning. One of our wonderful shots, a marine
named Fisher, who was stationed on the Wall,
was shot and instantly killed this morning, and
to-day really seems to be the most disheartening
morning of the siege, for so many men are going,
as the French Canadians would say, " on their last
great trail," or " over the Great Divide."

About 8.30 this morning, after our mess had
been straightened up, I was *en route* for the hospital,
carrying a pot of coffee to the doctors and nurses,
when some soldiers passed me, carrying a rough
litter bearing Captain Strouts, mortally wounded.
It was especially shocking to me to see him thus,
as he had breakfasted with us at seven o'clock, and
had seemed tired from his constant work, but
hopeful and in good spirits. His arm was hanging
limp, the hands and fingers stiff with agony. It
seemed but a moment before that I had passed
him at breakfast a cup of black coffee, to receive
which he had held out that strong, slim hand, with
the signet-ring on the little finger, and now it was
all so changed. In less than two hours the hand

was again being held out, but in his death-throes. He had been shot while going over to the Fu with Colonel Shiba and Dr. Morrison, to decide on some new plan of defence for that much-fought-over district, where the firing was constant. Dr. Morrison was hit at the same time, but not seriously, and the little Colonel had his cap shot off his head by two bullets.

These two wounded men were carried to the hospital, where Captain Strouts was attended to; but Dr. Morrison, owing to the great press of work, had to wait for some hours, nursing the exquisite agony of his wound, until his turn arrived. Poor Captain Strouts, with a cut artery in the thigh, only lived four hours, and died while asleep. He was so very, very tired. His work had been almost continuous night and day since he arrived from Tien-tsin, and especially hard, since he had to share the work and responsibility which necessarily fell on him by the death of so many officers. His death was very much felt by everyone. Dr. Morrison and Captain Strouts were frequent members of our mess, and in one day to have two leave thus—one wounded and one killed! Mrs. Squiers and I asked each other, " Who next ?"

GENERAL DEPRESSION

Can it surprise us that to-day the whole compound looks dreary and disheartened? So many deaths in one short twenty-four hours! I could write a great deal if it were of any use—of this compound, with the shot and shell and bullets, making it dangerous for us to move about the small open place in the Legation; of weary waiting for the troops through heat and rain; of great dread over the weak places in our defences; of crowded hospital and growing cemetery, and principally of the nervous strain caused by all this worrying and fearing over the fate in store for us should we arrive at that point when we could no longer hold our own. A good sergeant or corporal is missed as much when he is wounded or killed as an officer; it is especially true of our own marines, for in many instances they do the work of an officer, and take as much responsibility. The deaths are coming so frequently now that a final stand seems not improbable, and if when that is taken we continue to have the same percentage of deaths, then we can well say our prayers. It is discussed quietly by men that they will certainly kill their wives when that time comes. God grant it never may! Apropos of this, I have in my pocket a small pistol loaded with several cartridges, to use if the worst happens. A Belgian secretary stole it from the armoury for me—"in case you need it, mademoiselle."

Many is the time bullets passing through the tops of the trees have cut off branches or twigs which fall at our feet when attacks begin. We often see the flash of the cannon as it sends the shell over the compound, generally too high to do any damage, but passing before one knows it. And so it goes, shells and rifle-shots singing all around us. Late yesterday afternoon the shooting seemed to cease temporarily as I was sitting with Baroness von Ketteler on one of the benches which bore witness that this Supply Department had been, before the siege, the Legation tennis-court, when a bullet whistled with startling clearness within half an inch of my ear, passing between the Baroness and myself. Knowing that the sniper who had spied us was taking a moment to re-aim or reload, I immediately dropped from the bench on to the ground to get out of his range, trying at the same time to pull Baroness von Ketteler with me. This I could not do, and it was some time before one of the Customs students

PREPARING FOR EMERGENCIES

who was working quite near us realized that we were the target for this new sniping, and forcibly led her back to the Legation. In her agony of mind I am sure a bullet to end her suffering would have been truly welcomed.

We no longer talk about the troops. If they come in time they will come in time, and our one aim will be to last as long as we can. The only subjects of conversation now are the necessary strengthening of this or that barricade, the digging of trenches at this or that corner, to guard against the Chinese undermining us, as they are sure to do, mining being one of their favourite methods of warfare.

We are trying to prepare for all emergencies. People who, before the siege began, seemed to have reasonable intelligence, and, if one had thought about such a thing, looked as if they would show up pretty well if they were put to it, have now gone to pieces entirely, lacking apparently the desire even to appear courageous. The men often make some trifling ailment an excuse to shirk all work for the common defence, and spend their time groaning over the situation, and becoming more hateful daily to the men and women upon whom the real responsibilities of the siege are resting; while the women who have collapsed simply spend their hours, day and night, behind the nearest closed door, and await each fresh attack to indulge in new hysterical scenes.

I can honestly say there are more men to the bad than women. When anyone becomes really seized with this terror they lose all sense of proportion—the slightest provocation brings forth torrents of self-pity, and they ask only for the impossible. To-day I took the French governess her dinner, into which, I must admit, the cook had dashed the curry-powder rather too strongly. With this small *contretemps* as a starter, she seized my hands, and with heart-breaking sobs begged me to save her, as she knew, from the unusual taste of her food, that someone was trying to poison her. "Mademoiselle, je ne demande que peu, simplement qu'on me retourne tout de suite en France." To tell her we had all eaten the same curry, and that it was as impossible to send her to France as it was to send her to the moon, were words thrown away; she was hopelessly unbalanced with terror.

Several people have already lost their minds;

among them a dear old Italian priest, Père Dosio, the Superior of the Nan-t'ang, which was looted and burnt with the accompanying horrors. I talked with him from day to day, and from being at first *comblé* with grief at the ruin of his life's work in the destruction of his cathedral and hospital, he gradually has become full of hallucinations. His loss of mind has been a gentle affair compared to the violence shown by a Swedish missionary named Norregarde, who at times has to be confined with armed guards over him, as he is utterly deranged. He escaped once, and marched out of the British Legation gate to the canal, and it seems that he went direct to the Tsung-li Yamen, where he gave them, as far as we can learn by his own accounts when he returned, all the information they wanted, and especially urged them not to shoot so high, as few of their shots harmed us. Since his return he has been hourly guarded, but, unfortunately, we notice his advice has been taken, and Chinese shooting comes lower. The Chinese have a great respect for the insane, thinking the spirits who possess them are sacred. They gave him a good dinner, and he returned unharmed to the British Legation. The Chinese are working harder to take the Fu than any other point. It holds nearly three thousand native Christians, and it is these poor wretches whom the Chinese would first love to murder. Then, too, if they got the Fu, they could so easily mount guns on its wall and fire down on us. We *must* hold the Fu and the Tartar Wall directly behind the American Legation, but it will cost us the lives of all our marines to hold the latter.

On the 14th two messengers came to the British compound carrying a letter signed " Prince Ching and others." This communication was interpreted by some as a desire of Jung Lu to incriminate Prince Ching, as the letter came from the former's camp, and he is a well-known hater of both the foreigners and Prince Ching. If we answered it, and sent the answer to him to Jung Lu's camp, from whom it came, nothing would be easier than for Jung Lu to take the communication to the Empress-Dowager, and thus prove to her Ching's perfidy in writing to the Ministers.

Mr. Pethick disagrees entirely with this view, and urges the Ministers to answer it, as he feels convinced it is a genuine beginning of parleyings which, if nothing comes of them, would probably at least give us an armistice and a respite from the horrible attacks. This letter is fairly threatening, and it reads that we *must* now leave Peking, or they will do their *worst ;* that they have tried to communicate with us before, but their advances were never " gracefully received "; that we had fired first, and they were glad that so far only one Minister Plenipotentiary had been killed. As for the way of going, we must all leave Peking in tens, or those who desire to remain temporarily would be afforded protection and lodging in the Tsung-li Yamen, etc. It was addressed to Sir Claude and other Ministers, and they threatened in a postscript that terrible things would happen to us if they received no letter in answer by twelve o'clock the next day.

Opinions vary about it, but everyone agrees that it is worth while answering whether it is a ruse or not. So the response was sent yesterday at noon. The messenger who brought us this letter was the Chinese Christian who took, or tried to take, Sir Claude's communication to Admiral Seymour, and was caught by the Chinese, beaten in the most horrible way, and robbed of the letter containing information as to our numbers, strength, etc., which the Chinese must have been very glad to get. The messenger was then taken to Jung Lu's camp, where this letter was given him to deliver to us, as he knew the way that would get him quickly into our lines. This man was again used to take our answer to Jung Lu's camp. Some say the troops are on the way, and the Chinese are trying to start negotiations before they arrive, either to make us come out of our lines, so that they can murder us easily, or so that they can say to the Powers, when they finally arrive, that they kept up communication with us, and that it was our own fault that we barricaded ourselves in our Legations; others insist that it is altogether a *blague* and a *canard*.

The morning following Captain Strouts' death the Ministers and guard-captains unanimously voted Mr. Squiers to be Sir Claude's Chief of Staff, the position having been unfilled since Captain Strouts' death. The atmosphere of the besieged in Peking is not one of peace, but of bitterest feeling, especially strong against the British, and for no other reason than that the other nations begrudge the strategical superiority of the English position. Everyone hopes, with Mr. Squiers in this rôle, that things will run smoothly, and that perhaps Sir

FRIENDSHIP AND ENMITY

Claude's orders, when delivered to the different "guards" by an American Chief of Staff, and talked over with them in their own mother-tongues (for Mr. Squiers is a linguist), may be oil on the troubled waters. Let us hope so, for, should national feeling ever reach the top notch, this besieged area will separate—the Continentals on one side and the English and Americans on the other—and Heaven only knows how soon the end would come for everybody should this horror of military separation take place.

The strong feelings of friendship, that are perhaps due to the propinquity of our lines, have made the Russians our good friends and comrades, leading them to express to us freely their intense dislike of the British in violent phrases: "Ces chiens d'Anglais! Comment supportez-vous leurs arrogances et leurs manières de cochons?" And later on an Englishman would drop into our mess for a moment and admonish us with the words: "You Americans are the devil. You are on good terms with every d——d dago in the place; and as for the Russians, you love them as though they were your long-lost brothers!" It is unique, this feeling of ours of amity and good-will towards almost everybody here, and I am confident it is greatly due to the strong personality of Mr. Squiers that, as a Legation, we hold this extraordinary balance of things in Peking, which places the Americans in the lead on this diplomatic chess-board.

July 31.

In the afternoon of the 16th, the day of Captain Strouts' death, and while we were all attending his funeral, Mr. Conger, Mr. Squiers, and M. de Giers were told to come and interview a messenger who had arrived with a white flag, bringing a letter from "Prince Ching and others" in answer to our letter of the 14th. The messenger apparently came from the Yamen, and had a cipher telegram for the American Minister from the State Department in Washington, reading simply, "Give tidings bearer," then saying that we could send an answer to the Secretary of State through them; but, knowing it must be an open telegram, which they could easily change, no steps were taken to answer it. The following day came another letter from the Yamen to Mr. Conger that Minister Wu in Washington had written thus, "China is sent greetings and aid by the United States, and desires to know how is the health of Mr. Conger," and this message stated

EDWIN H. CONGER
(UNITED STATES MINISTER)

REPRODUCED BY PERMISSION FROM "THE SPHERE"

To face page 136

that the American Minister would be allowed to send one cablegram in cipher. Realizing the great responsibility devolving upon us to send a clear and strong telegram to the outside world, our Legation consulted with Sir Claude and other Ministers about the wording. The gist of what they sent was that, " We are holding our last position under shot and shell in the British Legation, and we will be massacred shortly if help does not come."

The following day, when the Yamen messenger came for the telegram, the other Ministers sent cipher messages also, hoping they might be sent. They were returned, however, with no apology. Since then there has been a message of some sort on every other day from the Yamen, signed " Prince Ching." The attacks are so irregular now that one cannot count on them, except that they are apt to occur at the most inopportune time during the day, and when least expected. Once, even two or three of the clerks or under-secretaries of the Tsung-li Yamen " called." They were evidently frightened and nervous at what they considered actually coming into the lion's den, but amenities only were discussed. We very naturally considered them of too inferior rank to treat officially. In one of the many letters in answer to Prince Ching's, Sir Claude wrote that we could hold out indefinitely with food, soldiers, and ammunition, but that the ladies and children felt the need of ice, eggs, and fresh fruit; so yesterday, the 20th, came three carts full of melons, six bags of flour, egg-plants, and an uneatable Chinese vegetable—no eggs, no ice, or fruit, except the unripe melons.

We have been trying to make a kind of market with the Chinese soldiers doing duty on the Chinese sentry lines, but although they would be very glad to pocket the big commission which they could get out of the transaction, they have not been allowed to do so by their officers, but they smuggle in eggs for us every morning at high prices (*bien entendu*), just enough for a very small supply for the hospital.

An interesting rumour that comes to us by a captured Chinese, and is generally credited to be true, is that Tung Fu-hsiang's army has retired south from Peking to meet the foreign troops. Another rumour, however, says that Tung Fu-hsiang nas departed westward, and as he was only a Mohammedan brigand before the Empress-Dowager elevated him to the head of her army, the Chinese think he has gone, not to meet our troops, but to continue the good work and merry life as a bandit in Mongolia. A letter comes to-day to Sir Robert Hart from the Yamen which is most polite and gushing. They regret most sincerely that his house and compound have been burned, and state at the same time that the Customs affairs have been turned almost upside down in consequence of lack of orders during the past six weeks from the Inspector-General. It is probable that they will come to Sir Robert for help as soon as things become more quiet.

The other day, when they sent us fruit and vegetables, they said they regretted they could not send us ice, because, if they attempted to do so, the Boxers, who like ice, would be sure to capture it. Apropos of ice, another baby's life could undoubtedly to-day have been saved had there been any in the compound. These "might-have-beens" are so agonizing.

M. Pichon, the French Minister, to-day had a very nice telegram sent him from France, saying: "You are unanimously voted to have the Legion of Honour. Your mother sends her love and greeting, and 15,000 Frenchmen are on their way to your support."

On the 18th a messenger got through from the Japanese Consul in Tien-tsin to Narahara, saying that he hoped the large foreign contingent of soldiers would get started by the 20th for the relief of Peking; he hoped there would be 24,000 Japanese, 6,000 Russians, 3,000 British, and 1,500 Americans; and that the Chinese city of Tien-tsin had been burnt, but not the foreign settlement.

The Russians seemed horribly worried about so many Japanese soldiers coming, but there are rumours that the Russians have been keeping away from Tien-tsin so as not to join the allied Powers, and perhaps be forced to make some promises which they might regret later, and that they are doing some seizing of territory at the present on their own account on the plea of defending their railways. An Englishman here, being, of course, anti-Russian, insists that this nation is absolutely careless about its Minister or the other Russian people trapped here, whether they live or not. If it is a question of making some coup for the aggrandizement of their country, they would not hesitate to sacrifice their people in Peking. One of the men in the Russian Legation is named Pompoff, and has a very pretty wife with a gorgeous

THE RELIEF REPULSED 141

voice, and as Russia is known to want Manchuria, he put it quite aptly in speaking of probable orders from St. Petersburg: "They will say, *Mon Dieu*, what is Madame Pompoff to Manchuria?"

A day or two ago, when news came to the Japanese that the allied troops were mobilizing in Tien-tsin, a letter came to M. Joostens, the Belgian Minister, from Kettles, the Belgian Consul, telling him in an excited way a little of the news we are all thirsting to hear—that Seymour's relief party had got near Peking about the end of June, but had been driven back toward Tien-tsin, owing to great numbers of Chinese soldiers opposed to them, and lack of supplies and water. They were then cut off from Tien-tsin by the Chinese under General Neih, and their whole column would have been massacred there had not 3,000 troops from Tien-tsin gone out to their rescue. Neih was defeated, and, in consequence, committed suicide.

The foreigners and soldiers then in Tien-tsin proceeded to take and burn the native city, over 700 being killed and wounded. Towards the end of this interesting letter Mr. Kettles naïvely remarked that he doubted if the Belgian Minister would ever get this letter, but if he did it might please him to learn that his home Government had wired to M. de Cartier to remain in Shanghai and await orders, for he undoubtedly would be sent to Peking as Chargé d'Affaires, "the Minister, M. Joostens, having been massacred." No matter what queer things happen in this world, humour is always left if one looks for it.

At the hospital an apparatus for applying X rays would have saved the lives of many. Poor Narahara, a Japanese officer, died this morning from lockjaw produced by a bullet which pierced his thigh. He has suffered horribly for three weeks. Dr. Lippitt, after waiting four weeks for his leg to be in a condition for the surgeons to make another search for the bullet, had the pleasant news told him, after an agonizing examination, that it could not be found. We are hoping that if the troops arrive soon their medical corps will have X-ray machines, and that Lippitt's leg may be saved. He has suffered and is suffering much physical pain, but more mental, I think, from the close proximity to the bed on which so many men have died, all the details of which he has seen, and the climax was reached during the night by the death of Narahara, whose wound was almost similar to his, although lately Narahara's wound has been complicated by lock-jaw, whereas in the doctor's case there have been no complications. If we get out of Peking, Dr. Velde deserves from every nation that is represented here a grateful acknowledgment of his services during the siege.

The wife of the Russian Minister, Madame de Giers, a handsome woman with a great charm of manner, has been a veritable angel of mercy in the hospital. She has personally nursed most of the Russian patients, for while all Russians of education speak either French or German, and the hospital nurses understand their wants, to the poor sailors, who can express themselves only in their own language, her nursing is a Godsend, and she is on duty with her suffering compatriots an incredible number of hours out of the twenty-four. A graduate trained nurse, working to make a record, could do no more than she is doing, and her physical strength, patience, and gentleness are a joy to witness.

No Minister's wife in Peking can approach in any way to having helped with the burdens of the siege as Madame de Giers. The old saw of

"Scratch a Slav and you find a Tartar" could be changed by those who see them here in Peking in so many instances "making good" to, "Scratch a Slav and you find a hero." The past week while these negotiations, communications, and messengers have been arriving the calm has been very noticeable, only I must admit that it seems almost as if one would prefer to say, "If it is war, then let it be war," for under these circumstances one would not, or, I should say, could not, have time to appreciate to the full extent this fiendish weather, this war and siege regimen, and the eternal and without end discussions about the troops. As long as the continual attacks were going on we knew it was a matter of life and death, and every man did his allotted work without a murmur, but now, owing to the half-armistice that exists, the five-week strain during this terrible weather is beginning to tell; everyone is seedy, and most of the work is done by dragging one leg after the other, while dysentery has a terrible hold on most of the people here. To me the most pitiful of all scenes in this compound is the collection of perambulators, huddled together in the shadiest part, with limp, languid babies in them, some looking so ill that their parents must feel

MORE NEGOTIATIONS

that each day more of the siege brings their little ones nearer death.

Yesterday, July 25, another communication came from the Yamen, saying that they again asked us to leave Peking, under, of course, their solicitous care; that they feel that they can no longer protect us, although in any circumstances they will continue to do all in their power, and that they would like all the Ministers to send open telegrams to their respective Governments that they are all quite well.

We suppose that the pressure of the world is being brought to bear on such high Chinese officials as can be reached to find out how we are, and they in turn are trying to force us to reassure our Governments by these covert threats. At ten o'clock this morning the Ministers had a meeting, and sent a unanimous statement, saying that Legations never send telegrams unless in cipher, so they could not comply with the Yamen's request, and that, as for wanting us all to leave for Tien-tsin immediately, we might consider the proposition if the Yamen would be kind enough to give us complete and accurate information as to what kind of a convoy they would give us, and what comforts would be furnished for the women and children. Of course, we have no idea of going *anywhere* with them as protectors ; but it is well to keep up communication, as it gives us time.

Surely it will be a surprise to the world to find us not dead, and to hear how we held our own. Last night the hospital statement was as follows : 165 men killed and wounded—12 per cent. killed, and 20 per cent. wounded.

People's larders are getting terribly empty, and the menu I quoted three weeks ago is now in the dim and distant past. We live quite sparingly, and are hungry most of the time. The chief comforts of our mess now are the Selzogene bottles that Mrs. Squiers brought with us from our Legation, in which we daily make enough soda-water to last throughout the day.

Last night I was walking round the compound with M. Knobel, a Minister Plenipotentiary, who has not seemed as yet to develop any special attributes during the siege beyond the very common one of being intensely hungry—so very hungry, in fact, that as we passed the bungalow given to the Russians, which boasts a few trees, Knobel's hungry eyes descried in the gloom six or more fat hens, be-

CHICKEN-STEALING

longing to some woman in the Legation, roosting high up on the branches. There was no sniping going on, and we took advantage of the quiet to walk once again round the compound, and noticed that, though it was early, everyone seemed to have turned in to get what rest they could before being awakened by the usual nightly attack.

The night was also getting blacker, and by the time we got round to the Russian bungalow again Knobel's fell purpose had seized him in a determined grip. He whispered to me, "If you will watch, I will get a chicken. There will be no noise, and to-morrow we will have a real dinner and eat that chicken." It flashed through my mind that at home, if clever darkies could not steal chickens without making a racket, I did not see how Knobel, who has probably never in his life come nearer to one than to pay his steward's bills, could expect to be successful. However, there was no time to argue. Knobel had left me standing in the road, watching his figure disappear in the darkness. A rustle, a slight squawk, and my Minister friend was by me again, with a squirming bundle under his coat. We ran, as if the Boxers were after us, straight to the Chinese courtyard, where we found our fat cook. Fortunately he had done his daily duty on the "gang," and was obviously delighted to receive our stolen booty—"All lighty. Me flixy good dinner to-mollow," and winked comprehendingly as he saw that Knobel had been holding Miss Chicken's neck so tightly she could not utter a sound. With a sigh of relief, Knobel turned her over to the cook, and with another but deeper sigh of anticipation of to-morrow's dinner, he steathily started by a roundabout way to return to his quarters.

Colonel Shiba, the Japanese commander, who has won the sincerest admiration from everyone, states to-day that he confidently expects the troops by July 28.

July 28.

This day, which was to have been so auspicious, brings us the worst news of the siege. It is to the effect that as late as July 22 no troops had yet left Tien-tsin for our relief.

A little Chinese boy, of the Presbyterian mission, aged fifteen, small but clever, was sent out by us, on the night of July 5, for Tien-tsin, with a letter to the British Consul, Mr. Carles, telling him of our very terrible plight, and how we must have

BAD NEWS

relief soon, and writing him in the strongest terms of our danger. This boy, after being let down over the Tartar Wall by a rope, made his way to Tien-tsin without many adventures, beyond being seized at one place and made to do coolie work for eight days. He then escaped, but, once arrived at Tien-tsin, he had great difficulty in getting through the outposts of the foreign troops who are apparently carefully guarding that part of Tien-tsin, which is in their lines. It is insisted here that the British Consul must be lacking in intelligence. He neither questioned the boy, who could have told him a great deal about our condition, nor did he give the boy any letters from the other Consuls, simply sending his own.

It took the boy a long time to walk back to Peking, and, finding the Water Gate too dangerous to enter by daylight, he waited until dark, and it was this letter that spread such a gloom over everything this morning. This communication of Mr. Carles was most unsatisfactory in every way, and the only excuse for this letter was that he was afraid it would fall into the hands of the Chinese. He wrote: "The rest of the British contingent, under General Gaselee, coming from Singapore, are expected on the 24th. Most of the Japanese troops are in Tien-tsin, and mobilized. The Russians are only landing at Taku. There are many Chinese troops between Tien-tsin and the coast. If you have plenty of food, and can hold out for a long time, the troops will save you. All foreign women and children have left Tien-tsin, and plenty of soldiers are on their way to your succour." This was all very disheartening ; but we realize more than ever before how long we still may be besieged, and the consequent economy of stores which should be practised, and there is talk of commandeering all private food-supplies.

The last sentence of his letter was hopelessly confusing. We did not know whether the troops had already started, or whether he was speaking of the Singapore contingent. Most people now feel that no reasonable Foreign Office should take two months to get a military relief party ready.

August 1.

This is a piping hot day, 108° in the shade. Our principal conversation now is asking each other, " Is Colonel Shiba's messenger reliable ?" This man brings in almost daily to the Japanese camp the most cheerful and apparently accurate news that the troops are not far from Tungchou. If he is reliable, we may expect them very soon, but we can hardly believe his statements, owing to Mr. Carles' letter. This is simply another variation to our old song of the siege.

The day before yesterday a letter came to Sir R. Hart from the Yamen, asking him to be so kind as to send a telegram to London telling the people there of our safety, because the different Governments were clamouring for news of their Ministers, and if he (Sir Robert) would send this telegram, it would be received as truth by the world, but they could not allow the Ministers to use their own codes.

Sir Robert answered immediately that the Ministers were quite right to decline to telegraph without cipher, and that he distinctly refused to send any telegram of such a nature as to reassure the world, because if he telegraphed the truth, the world would be so horrified that they would not believe his telegram. Well answered, Mr. Inspector-General.

I had the good luck to-day of being allowed to go over our defences on the Wall, and saw all of our protective barricades while getting there. Baron von Rahden and Mr. Squiers took me, and, needless to say, it was most interesting and thrilling. The conditions I had heard discussed for nearly two months I can now understand by seeing them all. I could also now understand the all-pervading charnel-house smells which at times during the siege have almost caused us to faint.

On each defended barricade loopholes have been made so that we can see, to some degree at least, the enemy. In many instances the loopholes are arranged with small mirrors, as the Chinese snipers often hit even these peepholes when a sentry's eye is seen, so that this further protection has been deemed necessary.

I looked through one from a barricade in the Hanlin, and what I saw was what I might see in looking through the wicket-gate of a horror chamber at the Eden Musée in New York. A group of gorgeously-apparelled Boxers with their insignia were pitilessly caught by death in a mad dash at this barricade, and there they were, stiff and stark, nearly all in the furious attitudes of assault! Even the standard-bearer was stiffly and conscientiously gripping his gay-coloured pennant.

A couple were shot in the back as they had started to run, and were lying flat on the ground, but a dozen or so, making up the body of the attacking party, held these horrible life-like positions with the most incredible rigidity. The sentry tells us that this hideous, almost theatrically posed, death-group has been thus for a couple of days. The Chinese would not come for their bodies, we could not, and there they were to remain until the carrion-dogs finished them, or until they eventually decomposed.

The combinations of barricades here, there, and everywhere are glorious, especially on the Wall, and well they might be, as they are made out of the huge rocks that were used hundreds of years ago to pave this wonderful piece of masonry. To stand and look down from the Wall into the British compound makes one realize more than ever how delightfully easy it would be for the Chinese, if they ever manned this part of the Wall, to point their guns downward and annihilate us.

Forgetting this possible picture, let me look down and tell you what I see on this beautiful, sunshiny August morning. Before me lies what we could naturally call the *terre du siège*, and comprises the Japanese, German, French, Russian, American, and British compounds, all of which have their flags flying somewhere, although in most cases the original Legation flag-poles have been shot down. Then comes as a pretty piece of colouring, in contrast to the sacked, burnt, and charred Chinese houses, all that remains of the Hôtel de Pékin, with its collection of flags of all nations flying in seeming defiance from the upper windows.

Further up Legation Street one sees a dirty, tired-looking, slimy green canal, running parallel to the British Legation, with a strong and high barricade on the bridge that spans it, so that we still have communication with those Legations on the other side—namely, the Japanese, German, and French. Then between and around these oases of compounds one sees an occasional big tree which has escaped burning, and which makes the scene of desolation seem even more lonely and desolate. Hundreds of houses, half burnt, half broken up, and wholly uninhabitable, tell the story of how in those first horrible attacks at the beginning of the siege they were used by the Chinese as cover, and then looted

A GATE INTO THE IMPERIAL CITY

THE FORBIDDEN CITY

and burnt. A stray dog of the large wolfish, mongrel type that is so common in Peking can be seen picking his way about from place to place with the queer look and walk that seem to mark carrion animals.

Standing in the same place, but looking westward, one sees such a picture of beauty as one could never imagine even in one's most exquisite dreams—a song of green and gold, the fairyland palaces of the wicked old ogress, the Empress-Dowager, these ideal gold-topped pavilions, palaces, and pagodas rising out of a veritable sea of green, which quivers and shimmers in the warm summer sunlight. In the old days we were frankly told that it was dangerous to wander too near enchanted palaces, and if this warning had been remembered, Kings and Queens would not have sent their knights of diplomacy to live on the other side of the Wall of this mysterious "Forbidden Purple City." It was always a hazardous thing to do, even in fairy stories, and it seems as if the tale of what happened to these misguided knights may finish in the regular good old way, "And they were eaten up and never seen any more."

August 2.

To-day there is posted on the Bell Tower—a sort of summer-house in the centre of the British compound, where all notices are posted, and around which people congregate at all times to hear the news—the translation of the cipher letter that came yesterday to Sir R. Hart, which came from the Customs in London, through the Yamen: " Keep up heart. Chinese finally routed at Tientsin on July 15. Troops having great difficulty in getting enough transports, but expect to leave for Peking after July 28. Is Chinese Government protecting you, and do you get food from them?" They then refer to Mr. Conger's telegram of the 18th.

Another choice bit of news comes to-day that two members of the Yamen have just been beheaded because they are suspected of being pro-foreign—Hsu Ching Cheng, Director of the Imperial University and President of the Manchurian Railway, at one time Minister to Germany and Russia; the other an ex-Taotai, a member of the Tsung-li Yamen, and an ex-Minister to Russia. Such is the price one pays in China for having assimilated broad ideas while enjoying diplomatic posts in Europe.

RATIONS REDUCED

As I write, over in Mrs. Squiers's house in the American Legation, where since this half-armistice we have been allowed to come occasionally and take a bath or read, I can see them taking away one of Mr. Squiers's favourite ponies to be slaughtered to-morrow. The supply of horses is getting very low, and it will certainly be hard for the fighting-men when the rations are reduced from horse and rice simply to rice, but it is really not pleasant to see one's pet pony being taken off to help the supply.

August 3.

Good news came yesterday, late in the afternoon, by a messenger who was clever enough to get through the Chinese lines. He brought in five letters, mostly from the Consuls in Tien-tsin—from Consul Ragsdale to Mr. Conger; from the German Consul to Von Below, the German Chargé d'Affaires; from Mr. Lowry to his wife; from Captain Mallory to Captain Myers; and one for Sir R. Hart. These letters are most cheering, because they all prove that our troops must arrive soon, but they are stupid, in that they give us none of the facts we are thirsting for; they don't even tell us approximately when we may expect relief.

They all take the attitude that the writers are pleased that we are not dead, then give us some trifling details about themselves in Tien-tsin and long, rambling accounts of what wonders they have gone through. Nine days besieged! and the carpenters are at work on the consulate porch, as a shell hit it; and Mr. Carles, the British Consul, even told us in the intricate consular cipher that he had had bad dreams about us the night before. The only letter that was to the point was from Colonel Mallory, an American, who sent us some good details and dates: the taking of Tien-tsin, July 15, etc.; the magnificent work of our marines; and last, but not least, his definite assurance that the Americans at least in the contingent would do all they could to start the advance-guard of 10,000 by July 28. General Chaffee's note to the American Minister seemed to promise good things from its very military brevity: " I arrived this morning. —CHAFFEE."

All the Consuls seemed overcome by the gravity of their own situation, for all the ladies have left or are leaving Tien-tsin. The night these letters came Von Below was sharing such dinner as we had with us. After it was over we all sat on the floor and discussed the comparative merits of the remaining stores, and he truly remarked that in these siege days, instead of looking at and discussing *bibelots* after dinner, one is glad to examine, exchange, and count tins.

August 7.

The day before yesterday an announcement was made in the *Peking Gazette*, the Imperial newspaper organ of the capital (these occasional bits of information we get by bribing heavily some fairly detached Chinese sentry) to the effect that Jung Lu was appointed by the Empress to devise means of carrying out the order that all the Legations were to be escorted to Tien-tsin, and that he was to see that they were tenderly cared for, and that any annoyance given to them on their way to the coast should call forth an immediate punishment.

Then a letter came to us, stating that they (the Yamen) had had letters from all their Ministers in the different countries saying that the Governments wished their representatives to retire to the coast, and that Jung Lu had been appointed to escort us. We replied, as usual, that we desired first to communicate with our Governments on the subject, and we also enclosed cipher telegrams. Yesterday came an answer, saying that they had been sent, but, of course, with lack of telegraphic facilities from Peking, it will probably be a week before our home Governments get them. To-day Baroness von Ketteler took a simple tiffin with Mrs. Squiers. Her condition has been such that she has not had one night of natural sleep in the seven weeks since her husband's murder.

I am sure everyone is sorry for Lady Macdonald, with that enormous mess to keep going. The complaints that people actually have the impertinence to make at her table, loud enough for her to hear, got so bad that one day she rose from her chair and said: " I give you the best I have; I can do nothing better; and, what is more, let me remind you that what is good enough for the British Minister to eat is more than good enough for anybody here."

August 8.

It is just seven weeks to-day since we came here for a few days until the troops should arrive, and food is running very short. There is, moreover, scarcely any condensed milk in the compound. Another European baby died yesterday, simply

Copyright, Pirie MacDonald, New York

GENERAL A. R. CHAFFEE

BABIES AND A HEN

from lack of food. It lay in its little coffin looking so white and tired. Out of pity for the mothers the hospital steward makes little rough coffin-boxes for their babies. All mothers who have children and infants who are ill or weak seem fascinated by these pitiful funerals, and they all go to them.

There is a good, busy old hen who lays an egg every day. She is given an entire deserted courtyard in the American Legation, a part of which is not in use, and I have fed her personally, or seen that she has been fed, ever since I placed her there at the beginning of the siege. There are three babies here, ranging in age from twelve to eighteen months, who are slowly dying from lack of digestible food. I give an egg to each mother every third day. The eggs are beautifully fresh, and the horror of it all is that these agonized mothers know, and I know, that, could I give the egg to them each day, instead of every third day, their babies could probably live; but as I can't, I have to divide them, and I cry with the pity of it.

Unless the troops come soon it is dreadful to think of the fate of the Chinese Christians in the Fu. Until now we have been able to give them a certain amount of food daily, but we can only spare this supply a few more days. These poor people will be forced to choose between leaving the Fu, with an almost certain chance of massacre, probably of torture, and staying where they are and dying of starvation.

No description of this place can give an idea of it as it exists to-day. To turn to Doré's engravings in Dante's "Inferno" would help. Every tree in the Fu, and there are many, has been stripped of leaves by these starving people; the smaller branches pulled and the bark chewed off. Diseased or not, these wretched people have been forced to remain here all together, as there is no other place for them. Carrion crows and dogs are killed and dragged to the Fu by sentries whenever possible, and these ravenous creatures pull the flesh from their bones and eat it without a pretence of cooking. Every morning when the two horses are shot at the slaughter-house, for distribution to the messes, half of the inedible parts are eaten with relish by these starving people.

The heat is intense, the ground in the Fu is brown and hard, the children are naked, and the adults wear little, but one and all are enveloped with the agony of relentless, hideous starvation.

The white rice which we have used in the compound has been finished, and we now use the yellow or uncleaned rice, which is very sandy and gritty, and which even the coolies in ordinary times would never think of using. It is made into curries or eaten plain, but one has to swallow it in spoonfuls without closing one's teeth on it, or it would be too much like chewing sand.

To-day a letter came from the Yamen saying that Li Hung Chang had arrived in Shanghai, and that he would soon begin peace negotiations by telegraph with the Ministers in Peking. Not a word was mentioned about our leaving for Tien-tsin, nor an apology for the continued sniping at night, and the occasional attacks which make us realize the lie that we are being "tenderly cared for and watched over by the Empress." Apropos of this clever old statesman, Li Hung Chang, the story is told of him that when, after some months of hard work and successful diplomacy, he had completed the terms of the treaty of Shimonoseki with the Japanese after the China-Japan War of 1894, although the Chinese had been whipped, Li had procured a most advantageous treaty for his Empress, and while the ink was hardly dry on the document he procured an audience with T'si An, and after kowtowing the entire length of the audience-hall in great abasement, he finally reached her august presence and told her of the successful termination of the work she had entrusted to him.

All high Chinese officials are supposed to get plenty of legitimate "squeeze" out of their political sinecures, and expect no monetary remuneration from the Government or throne. At the end of the interview the Empress made a sign to him to indicate that he would receive a personal present for his services, which would be given him in the anteroom. Li Hung Chang had always been a great collector of Chinese ceramics, and his collections were promptly sold by him to the highest bidder at Christie's in London for many pounds sterling. He was, in fact, notorious for this weakness, and it was well known that he would sell anything he owned, provided the amount offered was large enough, from the Russian sable coat in his own wardrobe to the fine latest antique, delicate-tinted rose vase he had procured. On leaving the audience-chamber, his eyes sparkled when a large cloth-of-gold bag, containing some heavy article, was handed to him by a eunuch. He flew to his own palace, hardly able

THE EMPRESS'S JEST 165

to wait for his secretary, Mr. Pethick, who is one of the greatest connoisseurs on ancient Chinese art, to arrive and examine this new acquisition, which had come straight from the Empress-Dowager's treasure store. Some time was spent in a careful examination to determine the dynasty during which this treasure was produced, but the date of this especial paste was lost, with its other technical classifications. After a long time Mr. Pethick lifted it gingerly, placed it on a table, put himself in front of it, drawing a wrap around his shoulders, and slowly, very slowly, held his hands up to it, turning them in the attitude of warming them at a fire.

Chinese need few words. Li understood, and was heart-broken. This was a clever reproduction made in Paris, and the secretary warming his hands before it meant it was so fresh from the pottery furnace that he could still notice the warmth. Naughty old Empress, fooling her most faithful of servitors!

Last night there was a very severe attack, coming from all sides at once, and the firing continued for many hours. It is outrageous, considering the letters we get every day from the Yamen, declaring to us that they give orders to their soldiers daily that there must be no more shooting.

It seems as though this "Chinese diplomacy" may be successful, and they may succeed in starving us out first. By negotiating indefinitely with our Governments and Li Hung Chang in Shanghai, and having assured the Powers we are quite safe, with plenty of food, they may be able to keep us here starving. What a refinement of cruel Chinese diplomacy that would be!

In one of our letters to the Yamen we stated that we insisted on their opening a market for our use, but the letter in reply ignored the subject absolutely, simply saying that they enclosed some telegrams from our Consuls in Chefoo and Shanghai, etc.

These telegrams, again, I must add, were most tantalizing. They gave us no news at all, simply congratulating us on being still alive. It is stated that from the Tartar Wall enormous numbers of troops have been seen leaving Peking, and from messengers and coolies we learn that these troops are advancing to give battle to our foreign troops, and that only a few companies of Jung Lu's troops are left here to continue to make things lively for us.

Friday, August 10.

Notwithstanding the day, we have just received the best news that we have yet had. A messenger arrived from the troops, bringing two short notes, one from General Gaselee, the commander of the British forces, and one from General Fukushima, the Japanese commander, both stating that they have arrived half-way between Peking and Tien-tsin; that they have met enormous forces of Chinese at two places, and that by hard fighting they had completely routed them; that if they had no further opposition they hoped to arrive between the 13th and 15th of this month, but owing to the size of their army, they could not move as quickly as they wished.

The messenger who brought the letter says that our long-distance artillery is what is terrifying the Chinese; their guns, though perfectly modern, are comparatively useless, except at moderate range. We are all wondering what our position will be until our troops arrive. Will the Tsung-li Yamen try and "save their faces" by continuing diplomatic relations, or will they feel that, with the foreign troops practically at their doors, they will receive no mercy from the advancing armies, and that they might as well try and kill us before it is too late to do so? Perhaps by violently attacking us at the last moment they feel they may succeed. Certainly, if several regiments of the defeated Chinese hurried on to Peking before our troops could arrive, they might make it a very near thing as to whether the next day we would hear our troops' buglers or the trumpets of the judgment-day.

For two nights the fighting has been constant, and the attacks general and fierce. The Chinese continue building their barricades higher and stronger; we have done the same, but we cannot understand how the Yamen can have the impertinence to speak of the present time as a time of truce and peace, with these attacks and fighting going on nightly, and making so much noise that the officers say it must be heard many miles out of Peking.

The Yamen claims that these shots are fired by people the Government cannot control, and that it is only sniping, which fact is absolutely ridiculous, as the Empress-Dowager, by cutting off the head of General Ma, for instance, could easily put a stop to it all. Such horrible dreams as one has now on going to sleep after a violent attack, and with the awful sounds accompanying such attacks still ringing our ears! The shrill cries of "Sha! sha! sha!" (Kill! kill! kill!) and the constant blowing of trumpets, is enough to account for our continued nightmares. While awake the brain can be somewhat controlled, but the real horror of our situation follows us even in our sleep. On awaking, one wishes one were asleep again, as the heat is something awful. The very worst weather of the year is upon us: the rain is almost incessant, and everything is sticky and muggy. Of course, this continual downpour is very hard on the soldiers, making everything a mass of mud, and the long, nightly attacks keep them out in the wet for hours. The flies, mosquitoes, and fleas are pests that still continue.

August 13.

An assurance came from the Yamen saying that we could have as much food as we wanted, and inviting us to send to them a list of what we desired, which we did, and they were to have sent the things yesterday by nine o'clock. Needless to say, they never appeared.

In the afternoon an official communication came from the Yamen saying in the most polite and abject Chinese that they would like a personal interview with the Ministers, to be held in the German Legation, as it was near their lines. This letter came late in the afternoon of yesterday, and the corps was to sleep all night on it, and decide this morning what to reply. In the compound feeling ran very high; everyone is against it. People felt that to receive these lying tricksters, who are offering peace and compliment with one hand, and with the other writing orders to their army to exterminate us, would be most undignified.

Early this morning the Ministers decided to bid them come at eleven o'clock to-day, the 13th. So they wrote to that effect, and the answer came back saying they regretted, but that other affairs and engagements of importance kept them busy to-day, so they would not be able to come, but hoped to give themselves that pleasure later. They also said that the terrible firing we kept up prevented them sending us the market supplies we desired. On the face of the awful attack of last night, continuing as it did from 8 o'clock until 6.30 this morning, the Yamen may have realized the absurdity of amicable chats, or perhaps they were

A FINAL EFFORT

afraid we would seize them, a measure seriously talked of by some of the officers. By seizing them all we could then let one depart with the cheering news that if the attacks continued the rest of the Yamen would be shot, but these clever old diplomats are not to be caught by any such old Chinese tricks.

August 14.

Such an attack as we have just had: incessant throughout last night, the entire night, by its continuousness and fierceness did much damage everywhere, but we answered back their volleys, and were for the first time during the siege spend thrifts with our ammunition.

August 15.

About midnight it appeared as though the Chinese were making a final effort to frighten and demoralize us by a terrific fire from all sides, and about one o'clock the pom, pom, pom, of machine-guns became apparent. To whom did they belong? Mr. Pethick had told Mr. Squiers that Li Hung Chang had bought fifty quick-firing guns just before the siege. In whose hands were they now? Did the Chinese still have them, or had they fallen into the hands of our relief?*

When these guns started their hammering there was a perceptible pause in the attack for four or five minutes, when the Chinese fire recommenced with redoubled effort, if such were possible, making a veritable ring of flame on all sides of our defence.

Through the racket that was around us all night we could faintly hear the unmistakable sound of the foreign guns of our troops. The dull boom of distant artillery—artillery coming to our rescue! We no longer asked each other, " When will the troops arrive?" We simply stood still, listening to this wonderful music, and goose-flesh ran up and down us. Early this morning the noise of battle gradually increased, and from the Tartar Wall we can see the advancing lines with their artillery,† which is answered by the Chinese on the Wall. The allies seem to be approaching Peking in every direction, for the Chinese are answering with cannon from every city gate.

* We found out later that the Russians had captured these guns, and were using them against the Chinese on the south-eastern corner of the Wall.

† Afterwards ascertained to be the Japanese trying to drive the Chinese from the Eastern Gate in order to enter the city.

THE RELIEF ARRIVES 173

We have all become like deaf people, and to make people hear we have to seize them by the shoulders and bellow into their ears. We don't quite know whether the Chinese will occupy themselves entirely with the advancing troops, or whether our fortified lines will be swept away by them in a last attempt on us before the allies thunder in to our rescue. Opinions vary; every barricade is doubly manned, as they have been, in fact, for the last two nights.

The Russians, English, and Americans finally succeeded in their attack on the south-eastern Wall, and entered the Chinese city almost simultaneously, marching along the southern Wall of the Imperial City towards the Water Gate, the Ch'ien Men Gate, and the Ha Ta Men Gate. The commanders received a cipher despatch from Sir Claude Macdonald advising them to enter the Imperial City by the Water Gate, as we held that portion of the Wall, and would be able to assist them in entering at that place.

At about half-past three I was debating with my maid whether I should or should not go over to the American Legation and take the cheerful bath which I had been indulging in each day lately.

Owing to the half-armistice existing, the early afternoon hours were fairly safe ones in which to move about the lines, and I was about to start with bathing paraphernalia and the little maid, when my inner consciousness was struck by something unusual happening out in the compound. I tingled all over, for my instinct had told me the troops had come.

Running to the old tennis-court, the only open space, I found everybody flying in the same direction. There were about two hundred Sikhs. They had entered Peking by the Water Gate, or what one should really call a drain, which allows the now dried-up water in the canal egress under the Tartar Wall. It is by this that our messengers have gone out and come in, and it is the route Mr. Squiers urged in his letter on both McCalla and Chaffee as being the only way by which troops could penetrate right into the heart of our lines without having to take any big gate of the Tartar city. These Sikhs came in this way, and they were the first to warm our hearts with the knowledge that this horrible siege is over.

It was queer to see these great, fine-looking Indians, in khaki uniforms and huge picturesque

THE SIKHS COME FIRST

red turbans, strutting around the compound, and as they entered right into our midst they all whooped a good English whoop. A little blond Englishwoman was so overcome at the relief really being here that she seized the first one she could get to and threw her arms around him and embraced him. The Sikh was dumfounded at a *mem-sahib* apparently so far forgetting all caste. It seemed odd that the word "relief" should have been personified in these Eastern and heathen-looking Sikhs, but it was all the more in keeping with this extraordinary siege in Peking that they should be the first on the scene to rescue us.

At this wonderful moment the Chevalier de Melotte, Mrs. Squiers, and myself, without a word spoken, flew with common consent to the point in our lines down Legation Street where we knew we could see the entering columns. Cannons were booming in all directions, caused by the Powers trying to enter by the different gates, shells exploding and sniping everywhere. We took our stand at the bridge crossing the canal, from where we saw large quantities of soldiers, sometimes even cavalry, come through the Water Gate. We had scarcely caught from this rather exposed point a bird's-eye view of it all, when a squad of Sikhs passed us with an officer of high rank, who turned out to be General Gaselee, riding in the midst of them. He jumped off his horse on seeing us, and showing on every inch of him the wear and tear of an eighty-mile midsummer relief march, he took our hands, and with tears in his eyes said, "'Thank God, men, here are two women alive," and he most reverently kissed Mrs. Squiers on the forehead.

It was so good to see him and meet him in this way. As soon as the despatch had arrived saying that General Gaselee was to be in command of the British forces, a smart-looking photograph of him that someone had cut from a magazine had been pinned on the Bell Tower, and it was so smart-looking, and his appearance so correct, that one of necessity lost interest in his personality; and now to see him thus—the military martinet all lost in this big-hearted, kindly man, who was almost crying because we were alive! A short time before meeting us, on his line of march, he saw poor Père Dosio's head stuck on the end of a pole, where the Chinese had placed it, and General Gaselee feared that this head might be but the beginning of a

Photo, Elliott & Fry

GENERAL SIR ALFRED GASELEE

To face page 176

STILL THEY COME! 177

series of Europeans similarly treated. We had considered the Italian priest so quiet and docile that he was not restrained at all, and yesterday he quietly wandered out into the Chinese lines, and undoubtedly he was killed before they knew his mind was gone, although at this stage the Chinese, I expect, were all too ferocious to have spared him even had they known of his dementia.

Coming to the "front" this way had to be paid for in a mild way, and a ricochetting bullet grazed my ankle, and one tipped the top of my ear. Chevalier de Melotte, our escort, had his cap shot off; but the battle lust had got into our blood, and it seemed that all this storm of bullets and dropping shells was but a new and exciting kind of hailstorm, and that to keep moving from one point to another was the one necessary thing to do.

The red-turbaned Sikhs and General Gaselee had come and gone, and now came long lines of yellow, khaki-uniformed Americans of the 9th Infantry, belonging to us, and General Chaffee, well set-up marines under Colonel Waller—they came on and on, stumbling through the hot August sunlight, line after line, without end, and we were nonplussed when they told us they were but a small detachment of the United States troops; and the tremendous storming of the Ch'ien Men Gate that was deafening us was being done by the Americans, who were having no easy time of it, as the Chinese were firing right down on them from their protected height.

Now this Water Gate entrance is no longer a drain, as it used to be, but is rapidly shooting forth a veritable military kaleidoscope. The yellow lines have changed into a stream of plodding, heavily-laden, tiny Japanese soldiers; then the picturesque uniforms of the French Zouaves, from Saigon, with their loose, baggy, cumbersome red trousers, come into view. We stood transfixed. It seemed to us as if the whole world had come to our rescue. Now the passing lines have changed again, and this time Cossacks, with their black, high leather boots and soiled white tunics, tramp past us, but we could not wait for more. We returned to the British compound, where we found that the galling fire from the Ch'ien Men Gate, which had done such damage amongst our attacking troops, had been stopped by a sortie of our marines down the Tartar Wall to the gate, where they silenced the Chinese and the Chinese guns, and helped our in-

A BRILLIANT CHARGE 179

coming soldiers to mount theirs in the erstwhile Chinese position, from which splendid vantage they fired directly into the Imperial City, and by this fire opened two more of the big gates of the Forbidden City.

This charge down the Tartar Wall to clear it of Chinese soldiers and Chinese guns by our marines was a brilliant bit of action. The guard, one and all, were anxious to help in some way our relief, which was so hard pressed at the Ch'ien Men Gate, and they welcomed with shouts of joy the orders from Sir Claude which enabled them to have a hand in this last great fight. They were joined by twenty Russians, the siege friends and almost the dear "bunkies" of our men, one Russian officer, and Mr. Squiers, of our diplomatic service (the Chief of Staff to Sir Claude during the siege), who led the charge.

The other nationalities have done about the same sort of thing on entering Peking; they have each taken some one gate, and are stationed now at different parts of the city, and, by a hasty conference of the generals and Ministers, they have each been given areas to be responsible for and to police. To police—which means that in these districts they will turn their men out to loot.

The Americans, after taking the Ch'ien Men Gate and the continuing inner gate directly up to the Purple City, left them manned, and then retired to the south-east portion of the Chinese city, which is contiguous to this district. In all Peking, but principally in our lines, confusion is rampant. This modern "Tower of Babel" will, I suppose, eventually settle itself or spread itself, as the case may require. One of the difficulties of late arriving columns trying to find their headquarters and marching round and round is the fact that their headquarters are also on the move, and until they bump into each other by accident they are at a loss to know what to do. To-day, at least, no one can direct anyone else.

Out of this wonderful military kaleidoscope, how glad I was to see old friends and acquaintances emerge! First to come to me was Colonel Churchill, the British Military Attaché to Japan, who got permission in Tokyo to come up with the Japanese troops to Peking. On finding me alive and well, he returned to the Japanese headquarters in time to send word with the first official telegram

NEWS OF THE OUTER WORLD

of General Fukushima to the War Office in Tokyo (announcing that the Japanese troops had arrived in Peking), to my brother-in-law, Lieutenant Key, who is the American Naval Attaché to Japan, that I was safe and well. How wonderful to think that, as the troops were marching up to Peking, the engineers were steadily placing the telegraph-wires, so that six hours after we were relieved a message went flying down to the coast with the tidings! To know that my dear sister in Japan and my family at home have been relieved from the uncertainty of my condition, already causes my heart-strings to loosen up a bit, and the tension is not quite so painful. A year before, I lunched with General and Mrs. Chaffee in Havana, and it was very nice to see him again here in this wicked old Peking.

He told me that no hours in his life had ever been so full of dreadful anxiety as the hours before the dawn of this morning at Tungchou, just before the starting of the columns for Peking. They could hear the continuous Chinese fire, and also the weak but steady spitting of our little Colt automatic gun, which he knew the marine guard had with them, and he said that all the sounds he heard spelled but one sentence, "Shall we be too late? Shall we be too late?"

It seems that the greater part of the allied armies had spent the night at Tungchou, and it had been absolutely settled by the commanders that the following night and morning hours were to be spent there, which would give time for scouts to go out and make reasonable reconnaissances; and that by early noon the main body of the allies should march on to Peking, each having a different city gate to take simultaneously. This plan was very nice and correct and military, but the Japanese and Russians, who had been eyeing each other distrustfully, could not stand it any longer, and throwing to the winds the pledge that they had given that day in conference, they both started their columns off double-quick before dawn for the capital. This breaking of their promise to the allies at the last moment, so to speak, rather mixed things up, but perhaps, after all, it was a relief to the others, because it then meant they were relieved, too, from any long concerted action, and they all could begin to march straight for Peking, which they did.

The night of the 14th was the last night that

our siege mess dined together on our little eight-sided Chinese table, which was generously stocked with the remaining tins which we had been hoarding for such a long time. Somebody has said, "There is a sadness about the last time of everything," and truly it was so with us. I felt exactly as children feel when they have been having a wild game of make-believe all day, when the grown-ups break in and say, "Come, children, there has been enough of this." And so it was with us: these terrible times are over, and there is nothing for us to do but remain passive, and try and get some sort of equilibrium into our lives again; and as we dined together last night there was a strong feeling, although we did not speak of it, that nobody but ourselves, who went through this incredible eight weeks of horror, were ever going to know really what the siege in Peking has been, and that we might all talk until doomsday, but the world will never understand. Perhaps it is too busy to try. So, as the kiddies say after a game, "Well, we know who's who, and who has done what, and that is as near as we ever will get to teaching the grown-ups, who know it all, about it."

August 16.

Captain Reilly, who was killed this morning while gallantly directing the fire of his battery, was buried this afternoon in a small open space in the American Legation. This funeral, however, was not as pitiful to me as the siege funerals we have been having all summer. Perhaps because there was some help and satisfaction to be got out of the military pomp and honours which were given him as he was laid away. All the guard captains were there. Captain Reilly's brother-officers and the officials in general assisted. The rough coffin was generously shrouded in an enormous flag, and after a short military service was let down into the wide, deep grave made for him.

Mr. Conger, as being the chief representative of things American in Peking, stepped down into the grave, and began to drag the flag from the casket, saying at the same time, "There are so few American flags in Peking, *this* one can't be spared." In a moment General Chaffee, the personification of justice for the dead and wrath for the living, shouted: "Don't touch that flag. If it's the last American flag in China it shall be

HOUSELESS AND HOMELESS 185

buried with Reilly." This man, whether addressing a Minister Plenipotentiary or an army division, is instantly obeyed, and so his dead subordinate was tenderly cared for by him at the end, and his body was buried wrapped in the flag for which he had given his life.

All of us, now we have no longer any right to continue living in the British Legation, feel that we should leave as soon as possible. The diplomatic people have houses to go to, and those who have no houses to go to are usually taken in by their colleagues, but the great majority are houseless and homeless.

It is like hunting a needle in a haystack to find a habitable house anywhere near the Legations, because, for blocks and blocks, almost everything is burnt. To find any decent Chinese houses one has to go too far from our lines to be really safe, as even now there are plenty of snipers still in Peking. Some wretched, dirty, and filthy temples have partially escaped burning, owing to the fact that almost up to the time that our troops arrived they were used by the Chinese as strongholds for themselves and Boxers. Into these holes people must go for lack of anything better.

Yesterday we spent the entire day moving from our tiny British Legation quarters to our own house in the American Legation compound, and such a difficulty we had in getting coolies to carry our many trunks and boxes!

The Chinese servants, almost without exception, were off looting or trying to find places for their families. They would not work, and it was not until 6.30 in the afternoon that we could hand over our two rooms to Dr. Poole. Mrs. Squiers is busy nursing little Bard; he has gone down with typhoid fever within the last few days, and we are all dreadfully worried about him. He is now at our Legation, in an isolated building. It is hard to nurse typhoid without fresh milk and ice, but we hope to get them before long. Mrs. Squiers is also nursing Captain Myers (who has developed a case of typhoid) and Dr. Lippitt, thus making two cases of typhoid in our little compound.

I had a chat to-day with Sir Claude Macdonald and M. de Giers, the Russian Minister, and both volunteered two highly complimentary criticisms of things American during the siege. One was that the services of Herbert Squiers had been simply invaluable during the most trying part of the summer; they both said—and surely, unless it was the case, these two people with such widely different points of view would never have both felt it—that he held both people and things together when people did not even dare whisper their fears to each other; that there might have been a possible division of forces during the siege owing to exaggerated racial feelings. The other criticism was that our marines lead in their intelligent work as soldiers. The accuracy of their shooting is extraordinary, and their ability to step forward, one after the other, on the death or retirement of an officer or non-commissioned officer and take his place is remarkable. They show the greatest aptitude to command, and are in no way disconcerted by the sudden increase of responsibility. In many instances which could be cited this was proved.

The British have never been known unnecessarily to sing the praises of other nationalities, and I was very happy to have this judge of things military tell me exactly what I felt and had seen from the beginning of the siege.

August 18.

Yesterday General Chaffee told me he proposed to send the first American convoy down the river to Tien-tsin on Monday, the 20th. A boat-load of convalescents and several boat-loads of missionaries will make up the convoy. Fargo Squiers, my maid, and I, will have our own little boat, and will be sent with this contingent for protection to Tien-tsin, where the Consul will be instructed to look out for us until we take passage for Japan to join my family.

Things in Peking are in a terrible state of chaos. Generals and Ministers know as little as anyone in the respect that they never decide on anything. Of course, they are awaiting instructions from home.

Yesterday I was *en route* from the British Legation to the American, when a big Sikh addressed me most respectfully, whacking his chest, which was bulging in tremendous curves: " Mem-sahib give me two dollars, I give mem-sahib nice things." There had just been an order issued to all British troops that the loot they procured each day must be turned in to some appointed official, so I fancied that this man must have wanted to get rid of something which he might find difficult to explain if found on his person. I, of course, had no money with me—it was the one thing we had had no use for for two months—but I returned to our Legation and procured two dollars, for my curiosity was aroused, and returning hastily to where I had left my man standing; and then, in the most evident perturbation, he unloaded what he thought was only a proper equivalent for the two dollars which he had asked of me—an exquisite gold-mounted cloisonné clock and two huge, struggling hens!

He was so anxious to be gone that before I knew it I had the clock in one hand and those wriggling old chickens in the other. They pecked at my hand, and I almost dropped them; but when one has been on short rations for two months one can stand without complaint a few difficulties in procuring food. The clock was a joy to look at, and the chickens were so big and so old; they made wonderful soup for the dear little kiddies, who, thank Heaven! are all still alive, but very much run down from the siege.

This morning Baron von Rahden came for breakfast, our conversation being, as usual, carried on in French. He told me he had procured for me a good sable coat—and when a Russian speaks of good sables they are good, for that nationality are expert judges of furs. I wanted to accept the coat in the spirit it was offered, as a testimonial of a charming friendship, formed under extraordinary circumstances, but owing to the intrinsic value of the garment I had to decline it. I don't think he understood very well my refusing it, and I had within an hour the pleasure of seeing him present it to another woman, who accepted it without a qualm, and without giving him, I thought, very many thanks. My soul was torn with conflicting emotions all day, and in the afternoon a Belgian, of whom I had seen a good deal during the siege, brought me a tortoise-shell bracelet, set with handsome pearls, which he had taken from the arm of a Chinese officer whom he had killed. I surprised myself by promptly accepting it. My nerves could not have stood it, and I took it rather than have a repetition of the sequel to the sable-coat episode.

When the rich Chinese inhabitants left Peking in such a hurry they in many cases took their treasure, their favourite wives and themselves out of the capital with the greatest expedition possible, while the young girls and women of their households thus left in countless instances promptly committed suicide, usually by hanging themselves, or drowning

THE QUESTION OF LOOTING 191

themselves in the wells of their courtyards. The men who are throughout Peking now looting, constantly run into these silent testimonials, showing how these people all preferred self-inflicted death to what they knew they could expect when the civilized and Christian soldiers of the West should be turned loose.

Yesterday a very animated generals' conference was held, the great question being whether there should be a unanimous effort to stop all looting and sacking, or whether it should be continued. The Japanese, French, and Russians were absolutely *pro*; English and Americans, *con*, the latter having the strictest orders from President McKinley against any looting. The English, although giving their vote for no looting, added they should continue to place "in safe-keeping all valuable things" found in the district given them to police. This, of course, gives them practically the right to loot, although whatever is brought in has to be placed in one place, where they have an auction later, and the officially prescribed amount *pro rata* is given to the officers and men, so that they are really doing just what the other nations are doing, only in a somewhat more legalized way. They say that these Indian troops, the Sikhs and the Rajputs, are something horrible when they get started, and occasionally the British officer who is supposed to always be on these parties sent out to procure "the valuable things for safe-keeping" has to shoot a man to keep them in discipline.

The rumours come in that now the whole of Peking is being looted, and worse, and each Legation, closed up in its little compound, feels like a little question-mark of respectability, surrounded by a whole page of wicked, leering horrors.

Our gates are all closed tight, and occasionally we hear thundering down Legation Street as whole troops of half-starved horses, ponies, and donkeys (animals which have been left by their owners in their stables, and which have managed by some means to free themselves, either by looters untying them, or perhaps fire freeing them), dash past at top speed all together in a fury of liberty regained. And dangerous it is for anyone to be on the road when one of these wild troops race down the street, for he will certainly be trampled to death. After a time these mad collections of animals become tame and quiet from hunger and

THE RESULT OF THE SIEGE: IN THE AMERICAN MINISTER'S HOUSE

Copyright, M. S. Woodward

THE RESULT OF THE SIEGE: FRENCH LEGATION RUINS

To face page 192

DEVASTATION

exhaustion, and are willing enough to be led into almost any courtyard. Everything is unusual in this wonderful Peking. This morning I walked with Colonel Churchill and Captain Mallory on the Tartar Wall and down it to the Ha Ta Men Gate. where we went down the Ramp and walked all over the tremendously exposed German and French lines with their barricades and defences. In the German compound the havoc wrought is unimaginable. Whole sides of the houses have been battered down, in some instances one or two walls only left standing; and as for the French compound, every house, every building, and every wall has been levelled to old Mother Earth again, and nothing but the little house of the concierge at the gate, which flies the French flag, is left standing.

On seeing this one can understand why the French at the conference not only wanted Peking to be looted and sacked, but to be burnt as well. As the whole place can be inspected now, Mr. Gamewell tells me that four big mines, almost completed, have been found, and, had not the allies arrived when they did, that the following night would have seen some terrific explosions in the British Legation, the Hanlin Library, and on the

Tartar Wall even. The mortality of the siege would thus have been doubled by twenty-four hours' further delay by our troops.

Baron von Ketteler's body was accidentally discovered on the 16th by the Russian troops who were passing near the Tsung-li Yamen, very near the spot where he had been murdered. The body had been thrown into an old wooden box and left. The polite communication which had been sent to the Baroness von Ketteler during the semi-armistice days of the siege that her husband's body was lying in state at the Tsung-li Yamen was thus proved to be an utter fabrication on their part. To-day his formal obsequies took place in the German Legation, the doyen of the Corps, the Spanish Minister, reading a short address, which was as well put as it was as hard for Baroness von Ketteler to hear. I did not go to the ceremony, however, for I felt as if I had attended more than enough to last me the rest of a long life.

Although the allies arrived on the afternoon of the 14th, it was not until the afternoon of the 16th that the Japanese troops went to the relief of the Pei-t'ang, where Archbishop Favier had held his own so long. They had had tremendous losses by

attack and mines which exploded in their midst—
300 Chinese converts killed, 75 orphan children,
and 60 foreigners, including 2 French officers who
had been sent with the 20 French marines to help
them at the beginning of the siege.

This huge fortified cathedral was the only other
mission in or about Peking which was strong
enough to hold out. At four o'clock they were
relieved, and at seven o'clock the French Minister
arrived to make inquiries about his compatriots.
All the commanders who have inspected the
Pei-t'ang say its defence was a wonderful one.

At every meal now Mrs. Squiers's guests are
most numerous, charming, and interesting. The
servants seem to be all back, and although the
days are filled with incredible stories of what the
different nationalities are "doing" in Peking, our
evenings are always delightful, as they are made up
of the companionship of the most delightful men in
Peking, who, when they arrive to dine, throw off
the disagreeable features of these war times, and
devote themselves with happiness to this opportunity, probably their first for many weeks, of
enjoying the ordinary cheerful amenities of life;
and while these nice parties smack of the camp—

for everyone is in uniform—it only makes things more interesting, for they help to cheer up the tired siege people. It is the same everywhere in the different Legations: each nationality is surrounded by its military, with a sprinkling of more or less unattached secretaries and Ministers Plenipotentiary, who are temporarily without Legations to go to or troops to attend to.

Sir Robert Hart is very busy with his mountain-high accumulated Customs work to be attended to, but he manages often to drop in to tiffin or dinner.

Colonel Mills, General Chaffee's Chief of Staff, an old friend of our host's, comes frequently to this hospitable house, as does Colonel Waller, a delightful person, with his young officers, Lieutenant David Porter and Lieutenant Harding. Colonel Mallory and Colonel Churchill, the British Military Attaché to Tokyo, who is an old friend of mine, and many other charming people, would make this list a long one should I attempt to make it complete.

Colonel Churchill is returning, as I am, as soon as he can to Tokyo. He intends to go down the river with Miss Armstrong and Sir Claude's little girls with the first convoy sent down by the

MRS. HOOKER, MISS ARMSTRONG, LADY MACDONALD'S LITTLE GIRLS, FARGO SQUIERS, AND COLONEL ARTHUR CHURCHILL

To face page 196

PLANS FOR DEPARTURE

British, which will be a day after General Chaffee sends down his.

Fargo Squiers, my maid, and I, will then meet him and Miss Armstrong and the children in Tien-tsin, and we will make our journey to Japan by the first way that presents itself. He thinks that Admiral Bruce, who is in command of the British fleet at Taku, will put a despatch-boat at our disposal, and that we will be sent immediately over to Yokohama.

In coming up to Peking Colonel Churchill brought me a very kind invitation from Admiral and Mrs. Bruce—I had known them for some time —to come to Mrs. Bruce at Wei Hai Wei, the British concession near Chefoo, in case I was ill or needed a rest before starting for Tokyo. So, with the letters to Colonel Moale, in command of our troops in Tien-tsin, to do everything possible for us, Mr. Squiers, Mrs. Squiers, and I, feel that Fargo and I will have an interesting and reasonably comfortable trip over to Japan, where I know my sister is counting the days until I return to her.

General Chaffee has delayed sending the first convoy down until the 21st, which gives me a little more time before starting. It has made me feel that really, after having been shot upon all summer from the Imperial walls, I should like a peep inside before I leave Peking.

The city has been portioned off to the different generals, and the English and Americans have a district where there is very little to loot. To-day a French officer of high rank, wishing to get treasure out of a palace that was in our lines, came to Mr. Conger and asked him if he would allow him to change the boundary a trifle. The Minister naïvely agreed to the Frenchman's purely disinterested request, and the consequence is there are a lot of indignant American military men wandering about trying to understand why this change in the map should have been made without consulting them.

August 19.

I talked over with Mrs. Squiers my great wish to see something of the wonderful Purple City before leaving, and while she was too busy nursing little Bard to go with me, she saw no reason why, with ample protection, and escorted by an officer, I should not ride through this mysterious and beautiful park.

AN UNNECESSARY REFUSAL

I had expected General Chaffee would give me an order to enter by the Ch'ien Men Gate and its continuing three gates, and pass practically through our own lines, upon his hearing that I wished to do so. He was usually so amiable when I asked him for anything, that this time, much to my surprise, he became very angry, and, pounding his fist on the table, he assured me that he would not allow me to even ride through the Imperial City, giving as his refusal the only reason that "there were sights of war there which no American girl should see," and pounding his fist a second time to emphasize the fact. All of which was ridiculous, as the sights of war referred to were simply the heaps of corpses which surrounded the different gates of the Imperial City by which the allies had entered, and, as a consequence of the defeat of the Chinese, the dead were still there. He was right, inasmuch as these are not pretty things to see; but as I had been in the midst of war for two months, and had seen all these things many times, I did not feel that it was just in him to deny me the privilege now of being able to get a bird's-eye view of this wonderful park, which he might have done by allowing a special permit to go round it on horseback before leaving. But one can't fuss with people who deny you things for what they think is for your own good, especially when the person in question happens to be General Chaffee.

After this sad refusal, the first person I met was Baron von Rahden, who, on hearing my tale of woe, was delighted to hear that it was one which was so easy to remedy. As General Chaffee had the power to write a permit to go into the Forbidden City, so had the Russian Commander-in-Chief. He flew off, and in a few minutes returned, bearing an order from the headquarters of the Russian troops giving him power to escort me through the Imperial City, with a company of Cossacks as a military guard, so that we could come to no possible harm from snipers or marauding parties.

I was all excitement to be off. I felt like a naughty child, and was afraid to stop a moment, fearing something might still stop me. But we could not start, as there was no horse or pony in the Legation, and the Cossacks had only their necessary number. Von Rahden was a resourceful person, and told me that while I was putting on a riding-habit he would have a horse got ready for me. He sent his men off with the word that

AN INTERESTING RIDE

some sort of an animal for me to ride must be here in fifteen minutes, and when I was ready to go I found the Cossacks all lined up and Von Rahden holding two of the sorriest, thinnest-looking horses I had ever seen. His men had stopped a stampeded troop of animals out in Legation Street, and these two were the best. The horse he selected was half mad with fear, but I finally managed to mount him, and off we started, lickety split, Von Rahden and myself leading, and the half-company of Cossacks thundering after us. This dashing down deserted streets and rushing up slight grades made me realize that one was no longer a prisoner, at any rate.

We rode for a long time through absolutely deserted streets, at all moments on the *qui vive* for shots from closed doors, or for a possible ambush at each turning in the road. Our horses shied at corpses in our path, and we were listening for unheard noises from apparently empty houses, many of which had tiny little foreign flags flying from some window or a painted foreign flag roughly executed over the door, the owners hoping these Western insignia might protect their property from looters.

Before entering the Forbidden City we passed through three series of walls, at the entrance to which were piled innumerable dead Chinese, silent proof that many lives were given in the vain attempt to protect the Imperial City; but after we were once inside, these horrors were forgotten in the grandiose landscape gardening, which almost overwhelmed us by its magnificent simplicity. We crossed the wonderful white marble bridges which spanned the artificial waterways, and the glorious lotus-flowers were all in bloom on the banks and partially in the water. They are such gorgeous, big flowers; they are like the Chinese architecture—wonderful in big, sweeping lines. We rode on through this semi-cultured landscape, where every detail was so carefully attended to that the ensemble was a complete joy to the senses, and after the eight weeks we had been barricaded in our Legation district this park seemed like heaven.

We climbed the Coal Hill, and got the only view I ever had of the Purple City. We were at such a height that we could look right down and get a good glimpse of the plan of these palaces, besides obtaining a gorgeous general view of the whole Imperial City. On descending the hill, I must say

COAL HILL

I was disappointed that the palaces in this Holy of Holies were not more imposing. They were low, long buildings constructed of the gorgeous Imperial yellow tiles. The extraordinarily rich colouring of these buildings made one forget momentarily the plainly low architectural lines. Unfortunately, we had no permission to enter these closely-guarded, mysterious precincts. We hated to leave this spot of beautiful trees, long avenues and vistas, and, above all, the pure air, to return to our half-burnt, wholly ill-smelling Legation district.

At nine o'clock all the Anglo-Saxons sang a *Te Deum* on the tennis-court. Mr. Norris conducted the service, and Dr. Smith, the author of "Chinese Characteristics," made a most stirring address. We all surely sang it with hearts full of a thankfulness we had rarely ever before felt.

August 20.

To-day I took a walk all over the German lines with Mr. von Bergen, Second Secretary of the Legation, and, in fact, all over our old siege lines, and said a cheerful good-bye to it all. To-night Mrs. Squiers has a farewell dinner, and to-morrow, at 6.30 a.m., we start with ourselves and our baggage in United States Army schooners *en route* to Tungchow, where we take primitive houseboats to sail down the Pei-ho to Tien-tsin. A detachment from the 9th United States Infantry is to accompany us, and everything is to be very military in this escort for the first convoy. How absurd to compare my coming to Peking and my leaving it! I came up on Sir Robert Hart's private car in a few hours, and will go down to the coast in an antiquated Chinese boat, which will take as many days as the train took hours. And so, floating down the river, I will have much time to think quietly about this wonderful siege, to forget the disagreeable and the bad, and to remember the great and the good.

INDEX

AMERICAN Legation. See Legations
Armstrong, Miss, 17, 23
Austrian Legation. See Legations

Belgian Legation. See Legations
Below, Von, Secretary to German Legation, 14; effect of siege on, 100
Bergen, Von, Second Secretary to German Legation, 203
Boxers, the, rising of, 7, 16, 23; captures of, 29, 35, 76, 152; outrages by, 38, 57
Brent, Mrs., 17
British Legation. See Legations
Bruce, Admiral, 197
Bruce, Mount, 2; ascent of, 4

Carles, Mr., British Consul at Tien-tsin, 148, 149
Cartier, M. de, 142
Cassini, Countess Marguerite, 5
Chaffee, General: arrival at Tien-tsin, 158; the relief of Peking, 177, 181, 199; a funeral incident, 184; the convoy to Tien-tsin, 187, 197
Chamot, Swiss proprietor of the Peking Hotel, provides food for the besieged, 114
Cheshire, Mr., American Legation, waiting for the relief troops, 15, 21; his bravery, 77

Ch'ien Men Gate, burning of, 25; firing of cannon from, 69; arrival of the relief force, 179
China, Empress of, and Prince Ching, 132; and Li Hung Chang, 163, 164
Ching, Prince, head of the Tsung-li Yamen, 69, 92; correspondence with the besieged, 132, 137, 138
Christians, Chinese, outrages on, 35, 38; located at the Fu, 75, 132; their want of food, 161
Churchill, Colonel, British Military Attaché to Japan, 180, 196
Cologan, Señor, Spanish Minister at Peking, 43; his illness, 120
Coltman, Dr. and Mrs., American physician at Peking, 20, 52, 79
Conger, Mr. and Mrs., American Minister at Peking, 52, 62, 120; message from the Yamen, 136; a funeral incident, 184; his naïveness, 198

Dana Collection, the, 14
Dosio, Père, the Superior of Nan-t'ang, his loss of mind, 131; Chinese outrage on, 176
Dutch Legation. See Legations

Favier, Archbishop, the Superior of Pei-t'ang, 37, 194
Feng-tai railway-station, 4; burning of, 8
Fisher, a marine, death of, 125

INDEX

Food-supply during the siege, 58, 73, 85, 106, 108, 109; an amusing incident, 146
French Legation. See Legations
Fu, the, Chinese Christians located at, 72, 132, 161
Fukushima, General, commander of the Japanese relief forces, 167

Gamewell, Rev., a missionary, a mainstay to the besieged, 112, 193
Gaselee, General, commander of British relief forces, 149, 167, 176
German Legation. See Legations
Giers, M. de, Russian Minister at Peking, 43, 120; message from the Yamen, 136; and the Americans, 186
Giers, Madame de, her wonderful help in nursing, 143

Hanlin Library, the, 107, 116
Hart, Sir Robert, Inspector-General of Customs, 13, 18, 50; death of Oliphant, 105; letters from the Yamen, 139, 151
Ha Ta Men Gate, defence of, 22, 33, 92
Hsu Ching Cheng, Director of Imperial University, 156

"International" cannon, the, 116
Italian Legation. See Legations

James, Dr. H., 75; murder of, 76
Japanese Legation. See Legations
Joostens, M., Belgian Minister, 141, 142
Jung Lu, communications with the besieged, 132, 134, 159

Kempff, Admiral, 14, 16, 17
Ketteler, Baron von, German Minister at Peking: Boxer incident, 24, 25; murder of, 45; discovery of body, 194
Kettles, Mr., the Belgian Consul, 141
Knobel, M., Dutch Minister at Peking, 43, 120; the chicken episode, 146, 147
Kroupenski, Mr., Russian Secretary, 23

Legations: Boxer outrages, 7 *et seq.;* arrival of the marines, 15; weakness of the American, 18, 31; waiting for the relief party, 21, 27; attempts to burn, 25 *et seq.;* alarming state of, 31; rescue of Chinese Christians, 35 *et seq.;* Chinese offer an escort to the coast, 42, 159; murder of Baron von Ketteler, 45, 194; strength of the British Legation, 48, 72; American women and children transferred to the British, 48, 50; American missionaries brought in, 49; life in, 50 *et seq.*, 119 *et seq.;* evacuation and burning of the Belgian, 56; attempt on the Dutch, 57; supply of food, 58 *et seq.*, 86, 108 *et seq.*, 160; in great danger, 61 *et seq.;* evacuation of Austrian and fright of the French, 63; general panic, 64; fighting the fire, 65 *et seq.;* the crowded hospital, 74, 90, 91, 102, 103, 105. 116, 142, 143; a sortie, 75; murder of Dr. James, 76; armistice, 78; renewed attacks on, 80 *et seq.;* attack on German, 92 *et seq.;* an unsuccessful sortie, 95; racial friendships and animosities, 95, 96, 121, 122, 135; Japanese valour, 97; boldness of the

INDEX

Chinese, 98; successful charge down the wall, 99, 100; funerals, 102 et seq.; discovery and successful use of an old cannon, 115, 116; plague of flies, 123, 124; Captain Strouts mortally wounded, 125; a bad day, 125 et seq.; wave of despondency, 129 et seq.; a missionary becomes insane, 131; communications with the Yamen, 132-134, 136, 145, 151, 159, 163, 169; Chinese send in food, 138; news of the relief force, 140; a chicken episode, 146; messenger sent to Tien-tsin, 149; description of the barricades, 151 et seq.; letters from Tien-tsin, 157; food running short, 160; more severe attacks, 165, 168, 171; good news, 167; arrival of the relief force, 171 et seq.; the question of loot, 191; the state of the German Legation, 193; discovery of mines, 193

Li Hung Chang, 163; and the Empress of China, 164, 165; purchase of guns, 171

Linqua Su, temple of, description of, 2; defence of, 9, 10

Lippitt, Dr., 34; wounded, 91, 142; typhoid fever, 186

McCalla, Captain, in command of the Japanese marines, 15; returns to Tien-tsin, 16; and the relief party, 21, 34

Macdonald, Sir Claude, British Minister at Peking, elected Commander-in-Chief, 120, 121; and Von Rostand, 122; communications from the Yamen, 132, 133; and the relief force, 173, 179, 186

Macdonald, Lady, and her children, 17; and Baroness von Ketteler, 46; lodges the American missionaries in the chapel, 50; food-supply, 85, 160

McKinley, President of the United States, forbids looting, 191

Magi-poo, rioting at, 14

Mallory, Colonel, sends news to the besieged, 158

Marines, the, arrival at Peking, 15; on the sick-list, 34; sorties, 35, 41, 99; death of Captain Strouts, 126; the relieving force, 179, 187

Martin, Dr. A. W. P., Director of Imperial University in Peking, 23; and the fire at the Legations, 68

Melotte, Chevalier de, his gallant defence, 56; arrival of the relief force, 175, 177

Merghelynckem, M., First Secretary of Belgian Legation, 56; saves the life of the French commanding officer, 117

Methodist Mission, burning of, 57

Myers, Captain, commander of the American marines in Peking, 17, 18, 21; makes successful sorties, 25, 99, 100; his hardships, 33; saves the Dutch Legation, 57; wounded, 103, 186

Mills, Colonel, General Chaffee's Chief of Staff, 196

Missions: arming of, 34, 35; removal into the Legations, 49, 51; work of Protestant and Roman Catholic missionaries, 57; burning of Methodist, 57

Morrison, Dr., *Times*' correspondent: his kindness, 9; stoned by rioters, 14; his advice to the Legation Ministers, 44; his hard work and cheerfulness, 69; and the Chinese Christians at the Fu, 75; wounded, 126

INDEX

Nan-t'ang, burning of the, 131
Narahara, death of, 142
Neih, Chinese General, defeat and suicide of, 141
Norregarde, a Swedish missionary, becomes insane, 131
Norris, Rev., English chaplain at Peking: the funeral of Oliphant, 105; works hard on the fortifications, 118; holds thanksgiving service, 203

Oliphant, funeral of, 105

Pei-t'ang, the, Roman Catholic fortress cathedral, 36, 37; relief of, 194
Peking — see also Legations: Boxer rising, 7 *et seq.*; burning of Feng-tai, 8; positions of the Legations, 12; telegraph broken, 21; assassination of the Japanese Chancellor, 22; burning of the missions, etc., 24 *et seq.*; fires in, 25 *et seq.*; description of, 26; treachery of the Imperial Chinese troops, 45, 47; burning of the Belgian Legation, 56; burning of the Hanlin Library, 71; entry of the relief force, 173 *et seq.*; looting, 192
Pethick, William, Li Hung Chang's private secretary, 11; his opinion of the state of China, 19, 20; his advice on the Yamen communication, 132; and the antique China episode, 165
Pichon, M., the French Minister in Peking, 43, 78, 87, 120; the Legion of Honour, 139
Poole, Dr., surgeon to the British Legation, 50, 52, 53, 59; the Legation fire, 68
Porcelain, antique, 14

Rahden, Baron von, commander of Russian Legation force, 25, 30, 96; and his undrilled soldiers, 110; the defences of the Legations, 152; the forbidden city, 200
Reilly, Captain, death of, 184
Roman Catholics in Peking, 36, 114
Rostand, Von, Austrian Chargé d'Affaires, 117; and Sir Claude Macdonald, 121
Russian Legation. See Legations

Salvago Raggi, Marquis, 43, 86, 120
Seymour, Admiral, 44, 51
Shiba, Colonel, Japanese commander at Peking: a sortie, 75; description of, 95, 148
Shimonoseki, Treaty of, 163
Squiers, Herbert, Secretary of the American Legation, 6; *en route* for Peking, 10; his collection of antique porcelains, 14; his hospitality, 15, 49, 73; beginning of the siege, 22; sends communication to Tien-tsin, 28, 29, 34; removal to the British Legation, 53; renovates an old cannon, 115; becomes Sir Claude Macdonald's chief of staff, 134; communications with the Yamen, 136; the defences of the Legations, 152; leads a sortie, 179; Sir Claude Macdonald's opinion of, 186
Squiers, Fargo, his brave adventure, 58; and the Legation fire, 68
Strouts, Captain, commander of the British marines in Peking, 18; a sortie, 25; Legation fire, 30; mortally wounded, 125
Su, Prince, 98

Taku Forts, taking of, 49
Tien-tsin, first relief force sent to

INDEX

Peking from, 15; message received by besieged from, 140; the capture of, 141, 158

Tsung-li Yamen, the Chinese Foreign Office, send a guard to protect the temple of Linqua Su, 6; Swedish missionary's interview with, 131; communicates with the Legations, 136 *et seq.*, 145, 159, 166, 169; send in food, 139

Tung Fu-hsiang, 51, 92

"Tungchou," the Roman Catholic church, burning of, 24

Velde, Dr., German surgeon at Peking, the excellence of his work, 73, 109, 113, 143

Waller, Colonel, 177, 196

Warren, Mr., mortally wounded, 124

Water Gate, entry of Sikhs through the, 174

THE END

BILLING AND SONS, LTD., PRINTERS, GUILDFORD

Some other Oxford Paperbacks for readers interested in Central Asia, China and South-east Asia, past and present

CAMBODIA

GEORGE COEDÈS
Angkor

MALCOLM MacDONALD
Ankor and the Khmers*

CENTRAL ASIA

PETER FLEMING
Bayonets to Lhasa

ANDRÉ GUIBAUT
Tibetan Venture

LADY MACARTNEY
An English Lady in Chinese Turkestan

DIANA SHIPTON
The Antique Land

C. P. SKRINE AND PAMELA NIGHTINGALE
Macartney at Kashgar*

ALBERT VON LE COQ
Buried Treasures of Chinese Turkestan

AITCHEN K. WU
Turkistan Tumult

CHINA

All About Shanghai: A Standard Guide

HAROLD ACTON
Peonies and Ponies

VICKI BAUM
Shanghai '37

ERNEST BRAMAH
Kai Lung's Golden Hours*

ERNEST BRAMAH
The Wallet of Kai Lung*

ANN BRIDGE
The Ginger Griffin

CHANG HSIN-HAI
The Fabulous Concubine*

CARL CROW
Handbook for China

PETER FLEMING
The Siege at Peking

MARY HOOKER
Behind the Scenes in Peking

CORRINNE LAMB
The Chinese Festive Board

W. SOMERSET MAUGHAM
On a Chinese Screen*

G. E. MORRISON
An Australian in China

DESMOND NEILL
Elegant Flower

PETER QUENNELL
A Superficial Journey through Tokyo and Peking

OSBERT SITWELL
Escape with Me! An Oriental Sketch-book

J. A. TURNER
Kwang Tung or Five Years in South China

HONG KONG AND MACAU

AUSTIN COATES
City of Broken Promises

AUSTIN COATES
A Macao Narrative

AUSTIN COATES
Myself a Mandarin

AUSTIN COATES
The Road

The Hong Kong Guide 1893

INDONESIA

S. TAKDIR ALISJAHBANA
Indonesia: Social and Cultural Revolution

DAVID ATTENBOROUGH
Zoo Quest for a Dragon*

VICKI BAUM
A Tale from Bali*

'BENGAL CIVILIAN'
Rambles in Java and the Straits in 1852

MIGUEL COVARRUBIAS
Island of Bali*

BERYL DE ZOETE AND WALTER SPIES
Dance and Drama in Bali

AUGUSTA DE WIT
Java: Facts and Fancies

JACQUES DUMARÇAY
Borobudur

JACQUES DUMARÇAY
The Temples of Java

ANNA FORBES
Unbeaten Tracks in Islands of the Far East

GEOFFREY GORER
Bali and Angkor

JENNIFER LINDSAY
Javanese Gamelan

EDWIN M. LOEB
Sumatra: Its History and People

MOCHTAR LUBIS
The Outlaw and Other Stories

MOCHTAR LUBIS
Twilight in Djakarta

MADELON H. LULOFS
Coolie*

MADELON H. LULOFS
Rubber

COLIN McPHEE
A House in Bali*

ERIC MJOBERG
Forest Life and Adventures in the Malay Archipelago

HICKMAN POWELL
The Last Paradise

E. R. SCIDMORE
Java, Garden of the East

MICHAEL SMITHIES
Yogyakarta: Cultural Heart of Indonesia

LADISLAO SZÉKELY
Tropic Fever: The Adventures of a Planter in Sumatra

EDWARD C. VAN NESS AND SHITA PRAWIROHARDJO
Javanese Wayang Kulit

MALAYSIA

ISABELLA L. BIRD
The Golden Chersonese: Travels in Malaya in 1879

MARGARET BROOKE
THE RANEE OF SARAWAK
My Life in Sarawak

HENRI FAUCONNIER
The Soul of Malaya

W. R. GEDDES
Nine Dayak Nights

A. G. GLENISTER
The Birds of the Malay

Peninsula, Singapore and Penang

C. W. HARRISON
Illustrated Guide to the Federated Malay States (1923)

BARBARA HARRISSON
Orang-Utan

TOM HARRISSON
World Within: A Borneo Story

CHARLES HOSE
The Field-Book of a Jungle-Wallah

EMILY INNES
The Chersonese with the Gilding Off

W. SOMERSET MAUGHAM
Ah King and Other Stories*

W. SOMERSET MAUGHAM
The Casuarina Tree*

MARY McMINNIES
The Flying Fox*

ROBERT PAYNE
The White Rajahs of Sarawak

OWEN RUTTER
The Pirate Wind

ROBERT W. SHELFORD
A Naturalist in Borneo

CARVETH WELLS
Six Years in the Malay Jungle

SINGAPORE

RUSSELL GRENFELL
Main Fleet to Singapore

R. W. E. HARPER AND HARRY MILLER
Singapore Mutiny

JANET LIM
Sold for Silver

G. M. REITH
Handbook to Singapore (1907)

C. E. WURTZBURG
Raffles of the Eastern Isles

THAILAND

CARL BOCK
Temples and Elephants

REGINALD CAMPBELL
Teak-Wallah

MALCOLM SMITH
A Physician at the Court of Siam

ERNEST YOUNG
The Kingdom of the Yellow Robe

*Titles marked with an asterisk have restricted rights.